A MANUAL OF BUDDHIST HISTORICAL TRADITIONS

(SADDHAMMA-SANGAHA)

A MANUAL OF BUDDHIST HISTORICAL TRADITIONS

(SADDHAMMA-SANGAHA)

TRANSLATED INTO ENGLISH FOR THE FIRST TIME

BY

BIMLA CHURN LAW, PH.D., M.A., B.L.

Fellow, Royal Asiatic Society of Bengal; Fellow, Royal Geographical Society; Honorary Correspondent, Archaeological Survey of India; Author, Some Ksatriya Tribes of Ancient India, Life and Work of Buddhaghosa, A History of Pali Literature, etc., etc.

GYAN

Published by

Gyan Publishing House
5, Ansari Road
Daryaganj, New Delhi-110002
Phone: 011-47034999, 9811692060
E-mail: books@gyanbooks.com

Distribution Network
gyanbooks.com
India, USA, Canada, UK, Australia, France

ISBN : 978-81-212-3755-0 (PB)
First Published, 1941

2nd Impression 2020

Printed at: Gyan Press, Delhi.

A Manual of Buddhist Historical Traditions
Author: Bimla Churn Law

A MANUAL OF BUDDHIST HISTORICAL TRADITIONS

(SADDHAMMA-SAṄGAHA)

TRANSLATED INTO ENGLISH FOR THE FIRST TIME

BY

BIMALA CHURN LAW, Ph.D., M.A., B.L

Fellow, Royal Asiatic Society of Bengal, Fellow, Royal Geographical Society, Honorary Correspondent, Archæological Survey of India
Author, Some Ksatriya Tribes of Ancient India, Life and Work of Buddhaghosa, A History of Pali Literature, etc., etc

PUBLISHED BY THE

UNIVERSITY OF CALCUTTA

1941

CONTENTS

CHAPTER VIII

CHAPTER IX

CHAPTER X

CHAPTER XI

A Manual of Buddhist Historical Traditions

INTRODUCTION

The Saddhamma-Samgaha which is a non-canonical Pali work of a later date has been edited in Roman characters for the first time by N. Saddhānanda of Ceylon and published in the Journal of the Pali Text Society for the year 1890. This work, as its title suggests, is a compendium of the traditional history of Buddhism. Its colophon mentions that the book was compiled by thera Dhammakitti of Ceylon at a great monastery called Lankārāma built by the great king Paramarāja.

The Saddhamma-Samgaha presents us with a bare outline of ecclesiastical and literary history of Buddhism drawn upon traditional materials. It is a historical record of the part played by Buddhism in Ceylon. The historical value of this work is enhanced by the inclusion of the account of two Buddhist Councils held in Ceylon during the reigns of Devānampiyatissa and Vaṭṭagāmini. As regards the three earlier Councils held in India, its account differs materially in some respects from those found in the *Vinayacullavagga*, in the commentaries of Buddhaghosa, and in two earlier Pali chronicles, the *Dīpavamsa* and the *Mahāvamsa*. This work also preserves very faithful records of the various Buddhist establishments of Ceylon, and it also contains important data for the chronology of Buddhist kings of India and Ceylon. A careful study of this book will surely give us glimpses into the history of Ceylon and her connection with India. After the third Buddhist Council was over, Buddhist missioneries were sent by thera Moggaliputtatissa to different countries for the propagation of Buddhism It was during the reign of Devānampiyatissa that thera Mahinda at the instance of thera Moggaliputtatissa went to Ceylon and with the kings' help and protection introduced Buddhism into the island of Lankā In this island the order of bhikkhunīs was first established by Therī Sanghamittā who went to Ceylon with the Bo-tree and converted the Queen Anūlā with her many female companions The account, however, is wholly based upon the *Mahāvamsa*. This book briefly deals with Buddhaghosa's life and his visit to Ceylon during the time of Mahānāma admittedly on the basis of the Cūlavamsa. The only new point recorded is that Buddhaghosa met Buddhadatta on his way to Ceylon. The author does not seem to be aware of the fact that Buddhaghosa himself states in the colophon of his *Vinaya Commentary* that he undertook and completed this work during the 21st year of the reign of king Siripāla of Ceylon. This work further gives an account of the compilation of the Pali commentaries and sub-commentaries of the three Piṭakas including other well-known Pali works by the theras. It also furnishes us with valuable information of Mahāvihāra, the Abhayagirivihāra, the Cetiyagirivihāra, the Lohapāsāda, the Thūpārāma, the Mahāmeghavanavihāra, the Pubbārāma, and other important Buddhist establishments in Ceylon. The last two chapters strike the keynote of the *Saddhamma Samgaha*. This book consists of eleven chapters which are summarised below.

The *Saddhamma-Samgaha* is written in an elegant and simple language. It belongs to the class of manuals and as such it is a mixture of prose and poetry In most cases the prose portion serves only as an explanation of the poetry portion. The author has borrowed very largely from the actual texts of the *Dīpavamsa*, the *Mahāvamsa*, the *Aṭṭhakathā* and other well-known Pali works which are simply referred to as *Porānā* or ancient authorities This manual contains many discourses common to the *Mahābodhivaṃsa*, the *Gandhavamsa*, the *Sāsanavamsa* and the like.

CHAPTER I After his enlightenment the Buddha lived for forty-five years. When he had attained the Parinibbāna, seven hundred thousand bhikkhus assembled there Thera Mahākassapa, recollecting the words spoken by Subhadda, felt the necessity of reciting the *Dhamma* and the *Vinaya*. Five hundred arhants were selected in order to hold a Council. After the rainy season, a little more than three months after the *Parinibbāna* of the Buddha, this Council was held at Rājagaha Thera Mahākassapa who was voted to the chair, took the preacher s seat, and asked questions touching the *Vinaya* and the *Dhamma.* Upāli recited the *Vinaya*, and Ānanda the *Dhamma.* The five hundred arhants recited together the texts in the manner in which they were presented and adopted. The work of the First Council was finished after seven months, and the collection of the *Vinaya* and the *Dhamma*, compiled by them, came to be known as thera tradition.

It may be noted here that according to this account, the three Pitakas with all their existing books and divisions were recited in the First Buddhist Council. It is, however, clear that the author has intentionally made a mistake here by stating that all the seven books of the *Abhidhamma-Piṭaka* were also recited in this Council. This statement is in direct contradiction to the statement (Ch III), that it was in the Third Council that Thera Moggaliputtatissa expounded Kathāvatthu in order to put a stop to all dissentient views. The remaining portion of this chapter is devoted to an elaborate discussion on the manifold division of the Buddha's word. This chapter contains nothing original.

CHAPTER II A century after the Parinibbāna of the Buddha, the Vajjiputtaka bhikkhus of

Vesālī promulgated the Ten Points which were not enjoined upon the bhikkhus. Thera Yasa, who was then staying at the Mahāvana, in the Kūtāgāra Hall heard it, and apprehending the danger in the Sāsana, the bhikkhus assembled. In order to hold a Council he selected only seven hundred arhants out of one thousand and twelve hundred bhikkhus who gathered there in a conference. These arhants met at Vālukārāma. Thera Sabbakāmi, questioned by Thera Revata, recited the Vinaya, and the dispute on the Ten Points was set at rest. The bhikkhus then recited the entire Dhamma and Vinaya. This Second Council was concluded after eight months.

CHAPTER III Two hundred and eighteen years after the Parinibbāna of the Buddha, sixty thousand heretics became envious of the gain and honour of the bhikkhus, and they, too, cutting off their hairs and putting on the yellow robes, went about the vihāras, disturbed the bhikkhus in their practices, and created nuisance in the Sāsana. So the bhikkhus were unable to hold the Uposatha ceremony for seven years. In order to purge the Sāsana of its blemishes, king Asoka called the bhikkhus in an assembly in the Asokārāma under the presidency of Thera Moggaliputtatissa. Then did the king question one by one on the doctrine of the Buddha. The heretics expounded their wrong doctrines and the king Asoka caused them to be expelled from the Order.

When the Sāsana was thus purified, the bhikkhus met and held the Uposatha ceremony. Out of sixty hundred thousand bhikkhus who assembled there, Thera Moggaliputta Tissa selected only one thousand learned and expert bhikkhus in order to hold a council. The Third Council was accordingly held at the Asokārāma. In that congregation Thera Moggaliputta Tissa expounded the Kathāvatthu, refuting the dissentient views. The bhikkhus recited the Dhamma and the Vinaya, according to the procedure adopted in the first two Councils. The work of this Council was finished after nine months.

CHAPTER IV After the Third Council was over, missionaries were sent by Thera Moggaliputta Tissa in bands each consisting of five Theras to various places to establish the Buddha's religion. Thera Majjhantika was sent to Kasmīra and Gandhāra, Thera Mahādeva to Mahisamaṇḍala, Thera Rakkhita to Vanavāsi, Thera Dhammarakkhita to Aparāntaka, Thera Mahādhammarakkhita to Mahāraṭṭha, Thera Mahārakkhita to the Yona country, Thera Majjhima to the Himalayan region, Theras Sonaka and Uttara to Suvannabhūmi, and Thera Mahinda with his four companions—Theras Iṭṭiya, Uttiya, Sambala, and Bhaddasāla—to the island of Lankā.

It was in the two hundred and thirty-sixth year after the Parinibbāna of the Buddha that Thera Mahinda reached the island of Lankā with four theras and a sāmanera named Sumana, and stayed on the Missaka mountain. On that day, in Lankā, a festivity called Jeṭṭhamūla took place. King Devānampiyatissa, came out of the city with a retinue of forty thousand men, and reached the Missaka mountain. At a place called the Ambatthala, he met Thera Mahinda. When they had come to know each other, they held conversation. The thera related the Cūlahatthipadopama Sutta, and the king with his forty thousand men came unto the three Refuges. Thereafter the thera related the Samacitta Suttanta at a great assembly of gods, and converted many devas, nāgas, etc. The thera, invited by king Devānampiyatissa, entered the city and the palace, and related the Petavatthu, the Vimānavatthu, and the Saccasamyutta. The king built the Mahāvihāra at the Mahāmeghavana-park, and dedicated it to the Order. Nine thousand and five hundred persons were converted at that time The king then built for the Order the Cetiyapabbatavihāra which the Order accepted. Aritttha with his fifty-five brothers received *Pabbajjā* from the thera, and became arahats

CHAPTER V King Devānaṃpiyatissa then caused the right collar-bone of the Buddha to be laid down in the Thūpārāma, and many people received Pabbajjā on that occasion. Subsequently a branch of a Bo-tree (taken from India) was planted with due ceremony, and on that day, the queen Anūlā with her many female companions received Pabbajjā from Therī Samghamittā. The king's nephew (sister's son) Ariṭṭha, too, with five hundred men received Pabbajjā at that time Under the direction of Thera Mahinda, king Devānampiyatissa then arranged for a council of the bhikkhus, and built a great hall in the Thūpārāma for the purpose. Many bhikkhus assembled in the Thupārāma. Thera Mahinda took his seat facing the south, Thera Ariṭṭha was seated on the preacher's seat facing the north. Sixty-eight theras headed by Thera Mahinda were seated round the preacher's seat The king's younger brother Thera Mantābhaya with five hundred bhikkhus was also seated round the preacher's seat. The remaining bhikkhus including the king and their attendants were seated in their respective seats. Asked by Thera Mahinda, Thera Ariṭṭha recited the Vinaya. In this way, they expounded the Dhamma and the Vinaya, and held the Fourth Council. The work of this Council began on the first great pavāranā-day in the month of Kattika, and ended in an indefinite time.

Chapter VI Three hundred seventy-six years after the Parinibbāna of the Buddha, Duṭṭhagāmini-abhaya became the king of Lankā. He built the Maricavatti-vihāra, the nine-storied Lohapāsāda, and the Great Thupa, one after the other, and duly consecrated them. He reigned for twenty-four years at Anurādhapura, and then died. Fifty-seven years after the foundation of the Great Thūpa, Vaṭṭagāmini-abhaya reigned in Lankā. This king built the Abhayagirivihāra and a great Cetiya and dedicated them to the Order of bhikkhus headed by Thera Mahātissa. Thereafter the Order of bhikkhus felt the necessity of putting down the three Piṭakas and the Aṭṭhakathā in writing. The bhikkhus expressed it to the king, and the king, at their request, provided them with a hall and other necessary articles for the purpose. The order of bhikkhus chose many thousand learned theras in order to hold a council. After rehearsing the Dhamma and the Vinaya according to the procedure adopted in the previous councils, the Order of bhikkhus caused the three Pitakas, with the text and the Aṭṭhakathā, to be written down in books from what had been orally handed down, and held it as the Fifth Council. The writing of the three Piṭakas was completed in one year.

CHAPTER VII Five hundred and sixteen years after the writing of the three Piṭakas, Mahānāma became the king of Lankā. At that time, a Brāhmana youth was born in the neighbourhood of the Bo-terrace in the Middle country of Jambudīpa. Skilled in all the sciences and versed in the three Vedas, he went all around Jambudīpa as a great disputant. He then came to a vihāra, and there he was met by Thera Revata who convinced him of the superiority of the Buddha's doctrine, and converted him to the Buddhist faith. The Thera then taught him the three Piṭakas. As he was as profound in his 'ghosa' or eloquence as the Buddha, they conferred on him the appellation of Buddhaghosa or the voice of the Buddha. In that vihāra, he composed an original work called the Ñānodaya, and wrote a commentary on the Dhammasaṅgani, called the Atthasālinī. Under the direction of Thera Revata, he started for Ceylon to study the Sinhalese Aṭṭhakathā, and compile a Paritta-aṭṭhakathā or general commentary on the three Piṭakas. On his way, he reached Nāgapaṭṭana, and there he boarded a ship. He, on his way, met Thera Buddhadatta on the great ocean, and held conversation with him. He reached the island of Lankā in the reign of King Mahānāma, and there at the Mahāpadhāna Hall in the Mahāvihāra at Anurādhapura, he met Thera Samghapāla. There he listened to the Aṭṭhakathā and the Theravāda, became thoroughly convinced of the true meaning of the Buddha's doctrine, and then sought the permission of the Order of bhikkhus to translate the Atthakathā. The Order of bhikkhus, for the purpose of testing his qualifications, gave him only two gāthās out of which he composed the commentary called the Visuddhimagga. The gods rendered that book invisible. He recomposed a second copy, and this, too, did the gods make invisible. When he recomposed a third copy, the gods restored the other two copies also Buddhaghosa, taking the three copies, presented them to the Order of bhikkhus. They found the three copies same in all respects, and rejoiced at his success. They gave him the texts of the three Piṭakas and also the Sinhalese commentaries. Buddhaghosa took all those books, and taking up his residence in the Padhānaghara on the southern side of the Mahāvihāra, translated all the Sinhalese commentaries of the three Piṭakas and of the entire Theravāda into Māgadhī (Pali). Thereafter, the object of his mission being fulfilled, he returned to Jambudīpa to worship the great Bo-tree.

CHAPTER VIII Six hundred and eighty-three years after the translation of the Aṭṭhakathā of the three Piṭakas, Parakkamabāhu became a sovereign-king of Lankā. One thousand one hundred and fifty-four years after the reign of Vaṭṭagāminiabhaya, he found the Sāsana decaying Under the leadership of Thera Mahākassapa of Udumbaragiri, he caused many hundred bhikkhus to be expelled from the Order, and made the Sāsana purified. He built many vihāras and cetiyas at Jetavana, Pubbārāma, Dakkhināiāma, Uttarārāma, Veluvana, Kapilavatthu, Isipatana, Kusināiā, and Lankātilaka. He then erected a great Uposatha Hall having nine stories and one thousand compartments, decorated with a tower, and rich in paintings, and creeper-works. He adorned the Jetavanavihāra with rows of Bo-trees, stūpas, cells, huts, halls and beautiful tanks and gardens. It was under his patronage that the Order of bhikkhus headed by Thera Mahākassapa compiled in Māgadhī the Atthavaṇṇanā of the Aṭṭhakathās of the Piṭakas. The following Atthavannanās (sub-commentaries) are mentioned by name :—

1 Sāratthadīpanī—The Atthavannanā of the Samantapāsādikā, the Aṭṭhakathā of the Vinaya.

2 Sāratthamañjusā (1)—the Atthavannanā of the Sumangalavilāsinī, the Aṭṭhakathā of the Dīgha-Nikāya.

3 Sāratthamañjusā (2)—the Atthavaṇṇanā of the Papañcasūdanī, the Aṭṭhakathā of the Majjhima-Nikāya.

4 Sāratthamañjusā (3)—the Atthavannanā of the Sāratthappakāsinī, the Aṭṭhakathā of the Samyutta-Nikāya.

5 Sāratthamañjusā (4)—the Atthavannanā of the Manorathapūranī, the Atthakathā of the Anguttara-Nikāya.

6 Paramatthappakāsinī (1)—the Atthavaṇṇanā of the Atthasālinī, the Atthakathā of the Dhammasanganı.

7 Paramatthappakāsinī (2)—the Atthavaṇṇanā of the Sammoha-vinodanī, the Atthakathā of the Vibhanga.

8 Paramatthappakāsinī (3)—the Atthavaṇṇanā of the Paramattha-dīpanī, the Aṭṭhakathā of the remaining five books of the Abhi-dhamma-Piṭaka.

This compilation of the sub-commentaries was completed in one year.

CHAPTER IX The text of the three Piṭakas contains one thousand one hundred and eighty-three chapters, innumerable syllables and letters. The whole Aṭṭhakathā of the Pitakas as expounded by Buddhaghosa, contains one thousand one hundred and sixty-three chapters, two lac nine nahuta seven hundred and fifty syllables, as well as ninety-three lac and four thousand letters. The Ṭikā of the three Pitakas contains six hundred and thirty-two chapters, one hundred and fifty-eighty thousand syllables as well as fifty hundred and fifty-six thousand letters. Other books, compiled by the theras, are then mentioned as follows :—

	Books	*Authors*
1	Visuddhimagga	Buddhaghosa
2	Kankhāvitaranī, or Aṭṭhakathā of the Pātimokkha	Buddhaghosa
3	Khuddakasikkhā	Dhammasiri
4	Abhidhammāvatāra	Buddhadatta
5	Paramatthavinicchaya	Anuruddha (in the city of Kāñcipura)
6	Abhidhammattha-saṃgaha	Anuruddha (in the city of Kāñcipura)
7	Saccasaṃkhepa	a disciple of thera Ānanda
8	Khema	Khema
9	Samghanandī	Kaccāyana
10	Samghanandī-Ṭīkā	Vimalabodhi and Brahmaputta.
11	Rūpasiddhi	Buddhappiya
12	Abhidhānappadīpikā	Moggallāna
13	Jinālankāra	Buddharakkhita
14	Jinacarita	Medhaṅkara
15	Paramatthamañjusā, a Ṭīkā of Visuddhimagga	Dhammapāla
16	Vinayasamgaha	Sāgaramati

No.	Work	Author
17	Nissayatthakathā, a Vaṇṇanā of Saccasaṃkhepa	Mahābodhi
18	Mukhamattakathā, a Vaṇṇanā of Paramatthavinicchaya	Mahābodhi
19	Paramatthadīpanī, a vaṇṇanā of Vimāna-Peta-vatthu	Dhammapāla
20	Subodhālaṇkara	Saṃgharakkhita
21	Vuttodaya	Saṃgharakkhita
22	Khuddakasikkhā-Ṭīkā	Saṃgharakkhita
23	Sambuddhavannanā	Saṃgharakkhita
24	Vinayavinicchaya	Buddhasīha
25	Kankhāvitaraṇī-Ṭīkā	Buddhanāga
26	Paramatthadīpanī, an Atthakathā of Therīgāthā	Dhammapāla
27	Abhidhammatta-samgaha-Ṭīkā	A disciple of Sāriputta
28	Dhammapada-Atthakathā	Buddhaghosa
29	Nettipakarana	Kaccāyana
30	Sāratthasālinī, a vannanā of Saccasamkhepa	A disciple of Sāriputta

Chapter X Thereafter the advantage of writing the three Piṭakas is related. The eighty-four thousand units of *Dhamma*, set up by the

Buddha, have by themselves taken the place of the Teacher as eighty-four thousand self-born Buddhas. Each letter in the Piṭakas should be considered as having merit equal to Buddha representation. Therefore, a wise man should write down the three Piṭakas or cause them to be written down in a book, or in a memorial in honour of the *Dhamma*. He who writes down the three Piṭakas, fulfils all meritorious deeds, and becomes free from all sufferings. He is reborn perfect in a higher life, and prospers always in happiness, wealth, enjoyment, fame, and the rest. He grows everywhere and in all respects. Even he obtains the *Sambuddhahood* and the most highest bliss of *Nibbāna*. Really speaking, this chapter sets forth the main purpose of this work namely giving encouragement to the transcription of the three Pitakas and the carving of Buddha's images. The source from which the verses are quoted as *Buddhavacana* cannot be traced.

CHAPTER XI The Sambuddhas have twofold body, one the glorious visible body, and the other the body of doctrine as preached by them. He who wishes his own welfare and greatness, should respectfully hear the preaching of the Norm. He who honours, esteems, reveres and respects the Norm is the person who honours, esteems, reveres and respects the Buddha.

The advantage of hearing the preaching of the Norm and of giving one's applause at the time of so doing is illustrated by a few stories, a brief summary is given below :

(a) Once the Buddha heard Thera Nandaka preaching the Norm and he shouted applause as soon as the preaching was over. Asked by Thera Nandaka, the Buddha replied that he had done so out of his great veneration for the Norm.

(b) A certain person, while with his seven sons returning from the forest, heard a woman singing a song relating to birth, old age and death. They too, on reflection, realised the three things, namely, impermanence, ill and non-soul, and attained the *Paccekabuddhahood*. Thereafter they became recluses, and went to a cave at the foot of the Nanda forest in the Northern Himalayas.

(c) Once the Buddha preached the Norm to the inhabitants of Campakā. A frog made the Buddha's voice an object of its thought, but it met with its death suddenly and was reborn in a big celestial abode in the Tāvatimsa heaven.

(d) Once, at the entrance of a cave, Sāriputta repeated the Abhidhamma-Piṭaka. Five hundred bats listened to his recital. They then passed away without taking any food and were reborn in heaven. They were again reborn in this world as comrades and entering the Order, became arahants, and reached Nibbāna.

(e) In the island of Sīhala, in a beautiful vihāra, named Uddalolaka-vihāra, there lived many deer, pigs and the like. A deer of that hermitage, while going to the landing place to drink water, heard the thera preaching the Norm. Then struck by a hunter it died and was reborn in the womb of the younger sister of Thera Abhaya, and afterwards obtained Arahantship.

(*f*) Once many merchants, desirous of going to the island of Laṅkā, boarded a sea-going vessel. As the ship went on peacefully, a bhikkhu who accompanied them, recited a portion from the scriptures. A great fish listened to the bhikkhu's recitation, but later it was killed by the people on the landing place.

In consequence of its listening to the recitation of the Bhikkhu, it was reborn in a wealthy family in the Rohinī country. He was later initiated as a monk and afterwards attained Arahantship.

In the following pages an English rendering of the text of Saddhamma-Saṃgaha has been attempted for the first time.

Honour to that Exalted One, Arahant, Buddha Supreme

CHAPTER I

The First Great Council

1 Having made obeisance to the Buddha, the Doctrine and the Order—the abode of virtue—I will present concisely the compendium of traditional history of the Good Faith.

2-3 Having completely wiped away (*i.e.*, removed) the obstacles by virtue of the merit (acquired) through services done to the Three Jewels, and having accepted the traditional accounts in the commentaries on the three Piṭakas in all their bearings, this is compiled by a wise man for the growth of the teaching of the Lord and for inspiring confidence among the copyists of the three Piṭakas.

4 Attend ye, all good men, present here, being willing to hear, to the presentation of the "Compendium of traditional history of the Good Faith," complete and clear.

To explain the matter, this is the connected story.

More than a hundred thousand aeons and four *asamkheyyas* (countless ages) ago, when our Lord, still *Bodhisatta*, had obtained the prophecy of the Twenty-four Buddhas (in succession), and had mastered equally all the Thirty Perfections, he reached the climax in his progress towards Wisdom.

Having lived for forty-five years after his enlightenment, formulated eighty-four thousand units of text, delivered to the other shore countless beings from the difficult path of existence and fulfilled all the duties of a Buddha till the ordination of Subhadda, the Wanderer, he passed away at Kusinārā, lying on the death-bed between the Sal trees

To this effect said the Ancients

5 "In olden times, the Great Hero, having offered homage to the twenty-four Sambuddhas, Dīpankara, and the rest, received from the prophecy of his (future) Buddhahood

6 When he had fulfilled all Perfections, and had reached the highest enlightenment, the sublime Buddha Gotama, set free the world from suffering [1]

7 When he had accomplished his duties befitting all Sambuddhas, and had reached the tranquil state, the Guide of the World, passed away on the bed of his Parinibbāna.

When the Exalted One, the Guide of the World, had attained the Parinibbāna, seven hundred thousand bhikkhus assembled there, and the

1 For verses 5-6, see *Mahāvamsa*, Ch I, vv 10-11

Venerable Elder Mahākassapa, senior of the congregation, recollecting the words spoken, seven days after the Exalted One had attained the Parinibbāna, by Subhadda, initiated in old age, addressed the bhikkhus thus: "Friends, we should recite the Dhamma and the Vinaya." The bhikkhus replied: "Reverend Sir, be pleased then to select the elder bhikkhus." Then the Venerable Mahākassapa selected five hundred bhikkhus who were arahants, and declared: "Friends, spending the rainy season at Rājagaha, we should recite the Dhamma and the Vinaya."

To this effect said the Ancients:

8 "Seven hundred thousand leading bhikkhus were among them, the thera Mahākassapa was at that time the senior of the congregation."[1]

9 Seven days after the Lord of the World, gifted with the Ten Powers, had attained the Parinibbāna, (the thera Mahākassapa) recalled to his mind the evil words of the aged Subhadda.[2]

10 To hold the Great Council the great Thera appointed to this end five hundred eminent bhikkhus who had overcome sins.[3]

11 On the second day of the second month of the rainy season, the bhikkhus met together in that splendid hall.[4]

1 *Mahāvamsa*, Ch III, v 4.
2 *Cf Ibid*, Ch III, v 6
3 *Ibid*, Ch III, v 9
4 *Ibid*, Ch. III, v 26

Now, on the second day, the elder bhikkhus, having finished their meals, getting ready with their robes and bowls, assembled in the meeting-place. When the bhikkhus remained thus seated there, the thera Mahākassapa addressed the bhikkhus: "Friends, which one should we recite first, the Dhamma or the Vinaya?"

The bhikkhus replied: "Reverend Mahākassapa, the Vinaya means the life of the Buddha's own. If the Vinaya lasts, the Order will endure. Therefore we should recite the Vinaya first."

Making whom the leader should Vinaya be recited?

"The Venerable Upāli," (they) replied.

The thera Mahākassapa chose himself to ask questions concerning the Vinaya, and the thera Upāli himself agreed to answer them. Then the Venerable Upāli rose from his seat, arranged his upper robe over one shoulder.[1] Paying homage to the elder bhikkhus, and sitting in the Preacher's seat, he took hold of a fan, inlaid with ivory. Then the Venerable Mahākassapa, seated in the thera's seat, asked the Venerable Upāli:

"Friend, where was the first Pārājika rule promulgated?"

"At Vesāli, reverend Sir."

"With reference to whom?"

"With reference to Sudinna, Kalandaka's son."

[1] i.e., the left

"In respect of what?"

"In respect of sexual intercourse."

Thereafter the venerable Mahākassapa asked the Venerable Upāli about the subject-matter, source, person, enactment, supplementary enactment, offence, and innocence as to the first Pārājika rule.

Just as to the first (Pārājika rule) so as to the second, third, and fourth, (Mahākassapa) asked about their subject-matter...innocence, the thera Upāli answered the questions as they were put to him Thereupon they arranged the Collection thus: "Let these four Pārājika rules constitute the *Pārājika* Section." They arranged the thirteen *Saṃghādisesa* rules under 'The Section of the Thirteen,' the two disciplinary rules under the section of the *Aniyata*; the thirty disciplinary rules under that of *Nissaggiya-Pācittiya*, the ninety-two disciplinary rules under that of *Pācittiya*; the four disciplinary rules under that of *Pātidesaniya* (those belonging to confession); the seventy-five disciplinary rules under that of *Sekhiya*; and the seven rules under that of *Adhikarana-samatha*[1] Thus they made the Collection of the *Mahāvibhanga*.

In the *Bhikkhunī-Vibhanga*, they arranged the eighteen disciplinary rules under the section of Pārājika, the seventeen rules under 'The Section

[1] For these terms a full discussion is found in B. C Law's *History of Pali Literature*, Vol I, pp. 51-60

of the Seventeen, thirty rules under that of *Nissaggiya-Pācittiya*, one hundred and sixty-six rules under that of *Pācittiya*, the eight rules under that of *Pāṭidesaniya* (those belonging to confession), the seventy-five rules under that of *Sekhiya*, and the seven rules under that of *Adhikaraṇa-samatha*. Thus they made the Collection of the *Bhikkhunī-Vibhanga*. In this way they also made the *Khandakas* and the *Parivāra*.[1]

Thus the two *Vibhangas*, the *Khandakas*, and the *Parivāra* making up the Collection of the Vinaya-Piṭaka, the thera Mahākassapa questioned, and the thera Upāli answered. At the close of questions and answers, the five hundred arahants repeated together the Collection in the same manner as it was adopted. When the Collection of the Vinaya was completed, the great earth quaked.

Then laying aside the fan, inlaid with ivory, and coming down from the preacher's seat, the venerable thera Upāli paid homage to the elder bhikkhus, and took the seat previously assigned to him.

To this effect said the Ancients :

12 "The great thera (Mahākassapa) laid on himself (the task) of asking questions touching the Vinaya and thera Upāli (was ready) to explain.

[1] This does not tally with the earlier account either in the *Culla vagga*, XI or in the *Sumangalavilāsinī*, I

13 Sitting in the thera's seat, the former asked the latter the questions touching the Vinaya; and the latter, seated in the preacher's seat, expounded (the matter).

14 And as the best master of the Vinaya expounded each (clause) in turn, all (the bhikkhus) knowing the custom, repeated the Vinaya after him." [1]

Then having made the Collection of the Vinaya, the venerable Mahākassapa wished to make the Collection of the Dhamma, and asked the bhikkhus: "In making the Collection of the Dhamma, making whom the leader should the Dhamma be recited?" The bhikkhus replied: "The thera Ānanda."

Then the venerable Mahākassapa chose himself to ask questions concerning the Dhamma, and the thera Ānanda himself agreed to answer them. The venerable Ānanda rose from his seat, and arranged his upper robe over one (*i.e.*, the left) shoulder. Paying homage to the elder bhikkhus and sitting in the preacher's seat, he took hold of the fan, inlaid with ivory. The thera Mahākassapa, seated in the thera's seat, questioned the thera Ānanda concerning the Dhamma:

"Friend Ānanda, where was the *Brahmajāla* [2] spoken?"

[1] *Mahāvamsa*, Ch III, vv 31, 33.
[2] *Dīgha*, I, pp 1-46.

"Reverend Sir, midway between Rājagaha and Nālandā—in the king's garden-house at Ambalaṭṭhikā."

"With reference to whom?"

"With reference to Suppiya the mendicant and his pupil Brahmadatta."

Now the venerable Mahākassapa also asked the venerable Ānanda the source and person as to the *Brahmajāla* Sutta.

Thereupon (Mahākassapa) asked: "Friend Ānanda, where was the *Sāmaññaphala* [1] spoken?" and so on.

"Reverend Sir, at Rājagaha, at Jīvaka's mango-grove."

"To whom?"

"To Ajātasattu, son of Vaidehī."

Now the venerable Mahākassapa asked the venerable Ānanda the source and person as to the *Sāmaññaphala* Sutta.

In this way, they rehearsed the *Dīgha-Nikāya* comprising thirty-four suttas beginning with *Brahmajāla*. Saying "Let this be called the *Dīgha-Nikāya*," they entrusted it to the care of the venerable Ānanda, and spoke thus: "Friend, please recite it among your followers."

Thereafter they rehearsed the *Majjhima-Nikāya* consisting of one hundred and fifty-two suttas beginning with *Mūlapariyāya* and entrusted it to

[1] *Dīgha*, I, pp. 47-86.

the care of the followers of Sāriputta, the captain of the Dhamma and spoke thus: "Please protect it."

Thereafter they rehearsed the *Samyutta-Nikāya* containing seven thousand seven hundred and sixty-two suttas beginning with *Oghataraṇa* and entrusted it to the care of the thera Mahākassapa and spoke thus: "Reverend Sir, please recite it among your adherents."

Thereafter they rehearsed the *Anguttara-Nikāya* comprising nine thousand five hundred and fifty-seven suttas beginning with *Cittapariyādāna* and entrusted it to the care of the thera Anuruddha, and spoke thus: "Please recite it among your adherents."[1]

Having thereafter rehearsed the *Khuddaka-Nikāya* (small discourse), divided into fifteen different treatises, to wit, *Khuddaka-pāṭha*, *Dhammapada*, *Udāna*, *Itivuttaka*, *Suttanipāta*, *Vimānavatthu*, *Petavatthu*, *Theragāthā*, *Therīgāthā*, *Jātaka*, *Niddesa*, *Paṭisambhidā*, *Apadāna*, *Buddha-vamsa*, and *Cariyāpiṭaka*, they put it (the whole collection of suttas) down, calling it the *Suttanta Piṭaka*.

Having thereafter rehearsed the seven different (abhidhamma) treatises, to wit, *Dhammasangani*, *Vibhanga*, *Dhātukathā*, *Puggalapaññatti*, *Kathā-vatthu*, *Yamaka* and *Paṭṭhāna*, they put it (the

[1] *Cf Sumaṅgalavilāsinī*, I

whole collection) down, calling it the *Abhidhamma Piṭaka.* Thus the thera Mahākassapa questioned about all that was rehearsed, and the thera Ānanda answered. At the close of questions and answers, the five hundred Arahants repeated together the collection. When the collection of the Dhamma was completed, the great earth quaked.

Then laying aside the fan, inlaid with ivory, and coming down from the preacher's seat, the venerable Ānanda paid homage to the elder bhikkhus, and took the seat previously assigned to him.

To this effect said the Ancients.

15 "Then the Thera (Mahākassapa) taking (the task) upon himself questioned about the Dhamma him (*i.e.*, Ānanda), the chief of those who had most often heard (the Buddha's word), him the treasure-keeper of the Great Seer (*i.e.*, the Buddha).

16 Likewise, the Thera Ānanda himself agreed, and taking his seat in the preacher's seat, expounded the whole Dhamma."[1]

The whole of "the Buddha's Word" is to be known as one by way of essence; as twofold by way of Dhamma and Vinaya; as threefold by way of first, middle and last, and so also by way of Pitakas; as fivefold by way of Nikāyas; as ninefold by way of Aṅgas; and as eighty-four-thousandfold by way of units of text.

[1] *Mahāvaṃsa*, Ch. III, vv. 34-35.

How by way of essence is it one?

All that the Exalted One spoke, by way of admonition or contemplation, to the gods, men, nāgas, yakkhas, and the rest, for forty-five years extending from the time of his gaining the highest wisdom up to his attainment of the Parinibbāna without leaving any residium for future existence, have only one essence, namely, the essence of emancipation. Thus by way of essence it is one.

How by way of Dhamma and Vinaya is it twofold?

The Vinaya-Piṭaka means Vinaya, and the remaining words of the Buddha constitute Dhamma. Thus by way of Dhamma and Vinaya it is twofold.

How by way of first, middle, and last is it threefold?

Herein

"Long I endured the cycles of rebirth,
Seeking but finding not the architect,
Rebirth continual is continual pain
But now have I espied thee architect!
Behold, thou shall not build the house again.
Broke are thy beams, thy pinnacle destroyed.
Now to Nibbāna[1] has my mind attained
And now in me all craving is destroyed."[2]

[1] *Visankhāra*—It means annihilation.

[2] *Dhammapada*, vv 153-54, *Jātaka-Nidāna-Kathā*, p 76. For translation, see *The Expositor*, p 22 *Cf Pss of the Brethren*, v. 184 (which ends differently), Rhys Davids, *Buddhist Birth Stories*, 103 f.

These were the first words of the Buddha. Some say: "In the *Khandhaka* (the Buddha) uttered a verse containing the song of ecstacy, namely,

'*Lo! when appear true doctrines to the saint,*'[1]

and these were the first words of the Buddha." But be it known that this verse contains only the song of ecstacy, produced (in the Buddha's mind) on the occasion of his attaining to the state of omniscience on the first day of the lunar fortnight, and reflecting on the mode of causal relations with his knowledge mixed with joy.

That which was spoken at the time of the Parinibbāna, namely,

"Hearken now, bhikkhus, I tell you: conditioned things are subject to decay; work out your salvation with diligence,"[2]

was his last word.

Between these two (events) all that were spoken (by the Buddha) form his middle sayings. Thus, by way of first, middle, and last it is threefold.

How by way of Piṭakas is it threefold?

All the words of the Buddha are divided indeed into three parts: the Vinaya-Piṭaka, Sutta-Piṭaka, and Abhidhamma-Piṭaka.

To this effect said the Ancients:

17 In them, by the Vinaya-Piṭaka is meant the Pārājika Section, the Pācittiyas, the *Vibhanga*

[1] See *The Expositor*, I, pp. 21 f.
[2] See *The Expositor*, I, p. 22.

of the bhikkhuṇīs, the *Mahāvagga*, the *Cullavagga*, and the *Parivāra*.

This is called the Vinaya-Piṭaka.

18 The collection of thirty-four suttas, divided into three books (*vaggas*), forms the *Dīgha-Nikāya*, the first in the order of enumeration.

19 The collection of one hundred and fifty-two suttas, comprising fifteen chapters, forms the *Majjhima-Nikāya*.

20 The collection of seven thousand seven hundred and sixty-two suttas forms the *Samyutta*.

21 Nine thousand and five hundred and fifty-seven—this is the number of suttas in the *Anguttara*.

22 & 23 The collection comprising fifteen divisions, to wit, *Khuddakapāṭha*, *Dhammapada*, *Udāna*, *Itivuttaka*, *Suttanipāta*, *Vimāna* and *Petavatthu*, *Thera-* and *Therī(gāthā)*, *Jātaka*, *Niddesa*, *Paṭisambhidā*, *Apadāna*, *Buddhavamsa*, and *Cariyāpiṭaka*, is considered as the *Khuddaka-Nikāya*.

This is called the *Suttantapiṭaka*.

24 & 25 The collection comprising seven divisions, to wit, *Dhamma-sanguṇi*. *Vibhanga*, *Dhātukathā*, *Puggala-paññatti*, the book named *Kathāvatthu*, *Yamaka*, and *Paṭṭhāna*, is called the Abhidhamma-Piṭaka, taught by the perfectly Enlightened One.

This is called the Abhidhamma-Piṭaka.

Thus by way of Piṭakas it is threefold.

How by way of Nikāyas is it fivefold?

There are five Nikāyas, to wit, the *Dīgha*, the *Majjhima*, the *Samyutta*, the *Anguttara* and the *Khuddaka*.

To this effect said the Ancients.

26 "Excluding the four Nikāyas beginning with the Dīgha, the rest of the Buddha's word is the *Khuddaka*."[1]

Thus, by way of Nikāya it is fivefold. How by way of Angas (types) is it ninefold?

All the words (of the Buddha) are classified into nine types, to wit, *Sutta*, *Geyya*, *Veyyākaraṇa*, *Gāthā*, *Udāna*, *Itivuttaka*, *Jātaka*, *Abbhuta*, and *Vedalla*.

"Herein, the dual (*Sutta*-) *Vibhanga*, *Niddesa*, *Khandhakas*, *Parivāra*, and the rest, the *Mangalasutta*, *Ratanasutta*, *Nālakasutta*, *Tuvatakasutta* of the *Sutta-Nipāta*, and other words of the Tathāgata bearing the name of Sutta should be regarded as *Sutta*. All the Suttas with verses should be understood as *Geyya*. In particular, all the chapters with verses in the *Samyutta Nikāya* form *Geyya*. The entire *Abhidhamma Piṭaka*, Suttas without verses, and other words of the Buddha not included in the eight types should be understood as *Veyyākarana*, or exposition. The *Dhammapada*, the *Theragāthā*, the *Therīgāthā*, those pieces in the *Sutta-Nipāta* not called Sutta and entirely

1 *Sumaṅgalavilāsinī*, I, 58, General Introduction · "Ṭhapetvā caturo p'ete nikāye Dīghaādike, tadaññaṃ Buddhavacanaṃ nikāyo khuddako mato'ti."

in verse should be known as *Gāthā*. The eighty-two Suttantas coupled with verses expressive of religious emotions should be understood as *Udāna*.

One hundred and twelve Suttantas introduced with the words: 'Thus was it said by the Blessed One,' etc., should be understood as *Itivuttaka* (lit. the 'Thus said') Five hundred and fifty birth stories beginning with the *Apaṇṇaka* constitute the *Jātaka* All Suttantas connected with wonderful and marvellous things spoken in this way: 'There are, bhikkhus, four wonderful and marvellous things in Ānanda,' should be understood as *Abbhuta*. All Suttantas in the form of questions asked through repeated attainment of delight and understanding, such as the Suttas · *Cullavedalla, Mahāvedalla, Sammādiṭṭhi, Sakkapañha, Saṅkhārabhājaniya, Mahāpunnama*, etc., should be understood as *Vedalla*."[1] Thus by way of Angas (types) it is ninefold.

How by way of units of text is it eighty-four-thousandfold?

To this effect said the Ancients

27 Eighty-two thousand from the Buddha, and two thousand from the bhikkhu (Sāriputta)—these eighty-four thousand Dhammas I have learned.

28 There are, in the Vinaya-Piṭaka, twenty-one thousand units (of text), in the

[1] See *The Expositor*, I, pp. 33-34

Suttanta-Piṭaka twenty-one thousand, and in the Abhidhamma-Piṭaka forty-two thousand.

Thus by way of units of text in explanation it is eighty-four-thousandfold.

"Of these, the Sutta containing one theme[1] forms one unit of text. The Sutta containing more than one theme forms more than one unit of text, and in such cases, units of texts are determined by the number of such themes. In verses, each query or question asked forms a unit, and each answer forms another. In the Abhidhamma, each tribal or dual classification, as well as each classification of conscious intervals, forms one unit of text. In the Vinaya, there are subjects, offence regarding the rules of conduct, tables of contents, classification of terms, interim offence, innocence, and division into triplets, wherein each portion should be understood as a unit of text."

Thus by way of units of text it is eighty-four-thousandfold.

The company of the self-controlled one, headed by Mahākassapa, recited the Buddha's word in these and various other divisions and arranged it after similar determination: "This is the Dhamma, this is the Vinaya," etc. And they rehearsed it in seven months. At the close of the Council the great earth, encircled by the ocean, quaked repeatedly, violently, with a vertical upheaval everywhere; and

[1] *Anusandhika*

[2] See *The Expositor*, I, p. 34.

various wonders manifested themselves, as though giving congratulations with well-felt delight at the thought: "The religion of Him who was endowed with the Ten Powers, has thus, by the thera Mahākassapa, been rendered capable of lasting a period of five thousand years.[1]

This is known as the First Great Council.

To this effect said the Ancients:

In this world,

29 "Whereas (this collection) was made by five hundred, therefore it was called 'That of the five hundred,' and whereas it was made by the Theras (Elders), it was also called as 'That of the Theras.'

30 Thus in seven months the compilation of the Dhamma, to save the whole world, was done by those (Theras) bent on the whole world's salvation.

31 'The thera Mahākassapa has made this religion of Sugata to endure five thousand years,'—

32 Rejoicing in this thought, at the close of the Council, the earth encircled by the ocean quaked six times.

33 Many wonderful signs were shown in the world in many ways. Now, since (the Canon) was compiled by the theras, it was called the Thera tradition.

1 See *The Expositor*, I, pp. 34-35.

34 The theras who held the first Council and had (thereby) brought great blessing to the world, having lived their allotted span of life, entered, all, into Nibbāna."[1]

35 Thus knowing that this life is transient and hard to win, be wise and exert yourself to attain the everlasting and immortal state.[2]

Here ends the Chapter, called 'The First Great Council, in the *Saddhammasaṃgaha*, compiled for the serene joy and emotion of the pious.

[1] *Mahāvaṃsa*, Ch III, vv 37-41, Geiger's *Great Chronicle of Ceylon*, p. 18.

[2] *Samanta-Pāsādikā*, p. 296.

CHAPTER II

THE SECOND COUNCIL [1]

Now, as days and nights, in succession, had passed, a century after the Parinibbāna of the Exalted One, the Vajjiputtaka bhikkhus of Vesālī promulgated at Vesālī the Ten Points.

Which were the Ten Points ? (They were) :—

"(1) That storing *salt in a horn vessel* (in order to season unsalted foods, when received), *was permissible* ;

(2) That taking the midday meal when the sun's shadow showed *two fingers' breadth* after noon, *was permissible* ;

(3) That *visiting the village* after meal, and there eating again (if invited), *was permissible* ;

(4) That *holding the Uposatha* separately by bhikkhus residing in the same boundary, *was permissible* ;

(5) That carrying out of official acts by an incomplete chapter, in anticipation of the *consent* of absent bhikkhus to be obtained afterwards, *was permissible* ;

[1] Cf *Cullavagga*, Ch XII, *Vinaya Texts*, III (*S B E*. XX, pp. 386 ff. *Mahāvaṃsa* (text & translation) Ch IV

(6) That it *was permissible* to do something *on the precedence of the preceptor's practice;*

(7) That taking *unchurned milk,* even after meal time, *was permissible;*

(8) That it *was permissible* to drink *unfermented toddy;*

(9) That the use of a *seat* not of the prescribed size, if it were *without fringe, was permissible;*

(10) That it *was permissible* to accept *gold and silver.*"

The king named Sisunāga, the son of Kāḷāsoka, was their adherent.

To this effect said the Ancients:

1 "At the end of the tenth year of Kālāsoka's reign a century had passed by after the Parinibbāna of the Sambuddha.

2 At that time many Vajjiputtaka bhikkhus shamelessly promulgated the Ten points at Vesālī." [1]

At that time the venerable Yasa, the son of Kākanda(ka), who was wandering through the Vajjian country heard: "The Vajjiputtaka bhikkhus of Vesālī are said to have promulgated the Ten points." And he arrived at Vesālī, thinking: "It is not proper that I, hearing the danger in the Sāsana of Him who was gifted with the Ten Powers, should live inactive, let me now expound the Dhamma, holding back the speakers of what is not Dhamma." There, at Vesālī, the

[1] *Mahavaṃsa*, IV, 8-9.

venerable Yasa, the son of Kākanda, stayed at the Mahāvana, in the Kūṭāgāra Hall.

Now at that time the Vajjiputtaka bhikkhus of Vesālī, on the Uposatha day, filled a copper pot with water and placed it in the midst of the Order of bhikkhus and said to the lay disciples of Vesālī who happened to pass by "Bestow on the Order a *kahāpana*, or half a one, or a *pāda*,[2] or a *māsaka*, or silver. It will be wanted for the requisites of the Order." All happened till there were in this rehearsal seven hundred bhikkhus, neither, more or less. So is this rehearsal of the Vinaya called 'That of the seven hundred.'[3] And in the (previous) conference one hundred and twelve thousand bhikkhus met together. In the midst of those bhikkhus, as the Thera Sabbakāmi, inspired by the venerable Yasa, the son of Kākaṇḍa, and questioned by the venerable Revata,—answered touching the Vinaya, the dispute on the Ten Points, [already] decided as desired, was settled.

Now the theras said "We will recite the Dhamma and the Vinaya" They chose seven hundred bhikkhus who were arahants, knew the three Piṭakas, and had attained mastership in

1 Name of a vihāra (monastery) See B C Law, *Some Kṣatriya Tribes of Ancient India*, pp 46 47

2 'One Pāda = ¼ of a Kahāpana, but double the value of māsaka'; hence 'each succeeding coin marks half the value of the preceding one.' *Pāli-Eng Dict.*, (P T. S), *s v.* Kākaṇika.

3 *Cf. Vinaya*, Mahāvagga, Ch XI, 1, 15; Ch. XII, 2, 9.

analysis. Just as the thera Mahākassapa had rehearsed [the canon], so did they sitting in the Vālukārāma and purging the Sāsana, again recite the entire Dhamma and Vinaya by way of Piṭakas, Nikāyas, Aṅgas (types), and units of text. This council was concluded after eight months.

To this effect said the Ancients

In this world,

3 "Whereas this council was completed by seven hundred, therefore is that rehearsal also called 'that of the seven hundred,' and because there was another held in time past this is called the Second.

4 & 5 The rehearsal was made famous by those theras who rehearsed it Sabbakāmi and Sālha, Revata, Khujjasobhita, Yasa, and Sānasambhūta, the six theras were pupils of the Thera Ānanda, and had beheld the Tathagata in time past.

6 Sumana and Vāsabhagāmi, endowed with knowledge, were pupils of the Thera Anuruddha, and had beheld the Tathagata in time past.

7 All those theras, however, who held the Second Council, had laid their burden, had accomplished their appointed tasks, and were free from the āsavas (sins).

8 Highly powerful were these theras, Sabbakāmi and the rest, and they, too, shining like the columns of fire in this world, attained the Parinibbāṇa.

9 Thus knowing that this life is transient and hard to win, be wise and exert yourself to attain the everlasting and immortal state '''

Here ends the chapter, called 'The Second Council' in the *Saddhammasaṃgaha*, compiled for the serene joy and emotion of the pious.

CHAPTER III

THE THIRD COUNCIL

Two hundred and twenty-eight years after the Parinibbāna of the Sambuddha, all heretics, numbering sixty thousand, being deprived of honour and patronage, so that they have not even enough to eat, sought that honour and patronage, themselves cut off their hair, donned the yellow robes, and went about the vihāras, entering even (the assemblies) at the time of the *Uposatha* and other services. They wrought diverse cankers stains, and nuisance in the Sāsana Therefore the Order of bhikkhus in the whole Jambudīpa for seven years did not hold the *Uposatha* ceremony.[1]

At that time Asoka, the righteous king, was consecrated fifteen years. The king, wishing to purge the Sāsana, of sins, called the Order of Bhikkhus together at the Asokārāma. In that congregation, the venerable thera Tissa, Moggali's son, being the senior of the Order, instructed the king in the doctrine. The king asked the teachers of other views, and discerned: "These are none of them (proper) bhikkhus but heretics." And

[1] *Points of Controversy* Commentator's Intro., pp 5 f., cf *Mahāvaṃsa*, VS. 234 82

having caused them to be expelled from the Order, he bestowed white lay-raiment upon them. Then the king said "Now, sir, the *Sāsana* is purged. Let the Order of bhikkhus hold the Uposatha ceremony." And,[1] providing a guard, he entered the city In concord the Order assembled and held the Uposatha ceremony.

To this effect said the Ancients

9 "Two hundred and twenty-eight years had passed from the Parinibbāna of the Sambuddha, when Asoka became king and lord of the earth.

10 Spending a week there in the pleasant royal park he (Moggaliputtatissa) instructed the ruler good doctrine of the Sambuddha.

11 In this same week, the monarch sent out two yakkhas, and assembled together all the bhikkhus on the earth

12 On the seventh day he went to his own splendid park and arranged an assembly of the Order of bhikkhus in its full numbers."

13 The king asked all the adherents of other views the false-believers, and knowing (their views), he caused them, in all sixty thousand, to be expelled (from the Order).

14 And the king said to the Thera (Tissa): "The Order is purged. Therefore, reverend sir, let the Order hold the Uposatha ceremony."

[1] For verses 10-22 see *Mahāvaṃsa*, Ch. V, vv 265-67

15 Providing a guard for the Order, he entered his fair city. In concord, the Order then held the Uposatha ceremony. [1]

In the midst of that congregation the thera Tissa, Moggali's son, presented the treatise, called the Kathāvatthu, refuting the dissentient views. Even as the thera Mahākassapa and the thera Yasa (had held a Council) so did he (the thera Tissa), out of sixty hundred thousand bhikkhus, select one thousand bhikkhus, who were learned in the three Piṭakas, advanced in the (four) Patisambhidās, and versed in the three kinds of knowledge, and the like, and did he recite the Dhamma and the Vinaya by way of Piṭakas, Nikāyas, Angas, and units of text Thus in reciting the Dhamma and the Vinaya, the great thera Tissa, Moggali's son, purged the Sāsana of all its stains, and held the Third Council. At the close of the Council the great earth quaked in many ways. This council ended in nine months

To this effect said the Ancients

16 "Even as the thera Mahākassapa and the thera Yasa had held the Dhamma Council, so also did the thera Tissa.

17 And in the Hall of this Council, the thera Tissa set forth the book, called the *Kathāvatthu*, for the future crushing of all dissentient views.

[1] For verses 14-15, See *Mahāvamsa*, Ch V vv 273 74.

18 Thus was this council of the Dhamma under the protection of king Asoka ended by the thousand bhikkhus in nine months." [1]

19 All those theras, too, holding the Third Council and doing many good to the world, lived until the span of their lives and then entered into Nibbāna.

20 Thus knowing that this life is transient and hard to win, be wise and exert yourself for the attainment of the everlasting and immortal state.

Here ends the chapter, called 'The Third Council' in the *Saddhammasamgaha*, compiled for the serene joy and emotion of the pious.

[1] For verses 16-18, See *Mahāvamsa*, Ch V, vv 277-279

CHAPTER IV

The Acceptance of the Cetiyapabbatavihara

Here this is the connected story.

The thera Tissa, Moggali's son, having held this Third Council, thought thus: "Where, in future, is the Sāsana to be well founded?" And on reflection he beheld: "(The religion) will be well founded in the western countries." Distributing the task among those bhikkhus he sent them, one here and one there. He sent the thera Majjhantika to Kasmīra and Gandhāra, (saying): "You will go to this country, and found here the Sāsana." With similar words he sent the thera Mahādeva to Mahisamaṇḍala, the thera Rakkhita to Vanavāsi, the thera Dhammarakkhita of the Yona country to Aparāntaka, the thera Mahādhammarakkhita to Mahāraṭṭha, the thera Mahārakkhita to the Yona country, the thera Majjhima to the Himalayan region, and the two theras, Sonaka and Uttara to Suvannabhūmi. He sent the thera Mahinda with his comrades, the theras Iṭṭhiya, Uttiya, Sambala, and Bhaddasāla, to the island of Lankā (saying) "you will go to the island of Lankā, and found there the Sāsana" And all who proceeded to different directions, went, each in a group of five only (because) in the western countries a company of five bhikkhus was declared to be sufficient for the purpose of ordination.

Hence to this effect said the Ancients

1 "The thera Moggaliputta, the illuminator of the religion of the Conqueror, bringing the (Third) Council to an end, looked into the future.

2 He beheld the founding of the religion in adjacent countries, and in the month of Kattika (Kārtika) he sent those theras, one here and one there.

3 The thera Majjhantika he sent to Kasmīra and Gandhāra, the thera Mahādeva he sent to Mahisamaṇḍala.

4 To Vanavāsī he sent the thera named Rakkhita, and to Aparāntaka (the thera) named Dhammarakkhita the Yona.

5 To Mahāraṭṭha he sent the thera named Mahādhammarakkhita, but the thera Mahārakkhita he sent to the country of the Yonas.

6 He sent the thera Majjhima to the Himalayan region, and to Suvannabhūmi he sent the two theras, Sona and Uttara.

7 The great thera Mahinda and his disciples—the theras Itthiya, Uttiya, Sambala and Bhaddasāla.

8 These five theras he sent with the charge: "You will found, in the delightful island of Lankā, the delightful Rule of the Conqueror?" "[1]

[1] *Mahāvamsa*, Ch XII, vv 1-8

Charged by his teacher and by the Order of bhikkhus. "You will go to the island of Lankā, and found there the religion," the thera Mahinda, however, pondered: "Is it the proper time now to go to the island of Lankā?" Then Sakka, king of the gods, approached the thera, and said thus "Reverend Sir, king Muṭasiva is dead; now reigns the great king Devānampiyatissa. And by the Sammāsambuddha have you been predicted 'In future, a bhikkhu named Mahinda will convert the island of Lankā.' Therefore, Reverend Sir, this is the fitting time to go to the excellent island I, too, shall be your helper."[1]

To this effect said the Ancients

9 "At that time the thera named Mahinda was the senior of the Order There were the four (other) theras—Itthiya, Uttiya, Bhaddasāla and Sambala.

10 And (there were) the miraculously gifted Sāmaṇera Sumana, mighty in the six supernormal powers, and the lay disciple Bhaṇḍuka, the seventh among them, who had discerned the truth.

11 They, like royal swans in the air, were sent forth from the island of Jambu. Thus the theras rose up and alighted on the most excellent city.

[1] *Cf Mahāvaṃsa* Ch. XIII, vv 1 2, 15 16, *Samantapāsādikā*, p 319

12 In front of the best city, on the peak of a mountain which resembled the clouds, they stayed, as do the swans high above in the sky.[1]

Let it be known that in the two hundred and thirty-sixth year after the Parinibbāna of the Sammāsambuddha the venerable thera Mahinda who had thus come with Itthiya, and the rest, and stayed on the Missaka-mountain, gained a footing in this island

And on that day, in the island of Lankā, the festival called Jettamūla, took place Announcing the festival and commanding his ministers : "Celebrate the festival," the great king Devānaṃpiyatissa came out of the city with a retinue of forty thousand men, and being desirous of enjoying the pleasure of the chase, went to the place where the Missaka-mountain was Now, a deity residing on that mountain thought "I will make the theras visible to the king," and assuming the form of a red deer, began to roam, eating the grass as it were, not far from the king. Then the king struck (a sound) at his bowstring. Along the way to the Ambatthala the deer began to flee. Pursuing closely, the king ascended the Ambatthala. The deer, too, disappeared at a place not far from the theras. When the thera Mahinda had beheld the king drawing near, he resolved : "Let the king alone see me, not others," and said : "Tissa, Tissa, come here."

[1] For verses 9-12, see *Dīpavaṃsa*, Ch XII, vv 36-40

On hearing this, the king thought: "There is none born in this island who can address me by my name, but this shaven-headed fellow wearing the yellow patch-work garment addresses me by my name. Who then shall be human or not human?"

The thera replied:

"Samaṇas are we, O great king, disciples of the king of righteousness. From compassion towards you are we come here from the island of Jambu."

As soon as the king heard the thera's word, he instantly laid his arrow aside and, while speaking in friendly term, took his seat on one side

As it has been said

"The king laying his arrow aside took his seat on one side, and as he was seated he exchanged friendly greetings connected with varied meanings."

At the very moment those forty thousand men came and surrounded the king. Then to him the thera showed the six other persons also When the king had beheld these, he asked "When did these come here?" "(They came) with me, O great king." "But are there now in the island of Jambu also other samaṇas like these?" "There are, O great king. The island of Jambu is now-a-days glowing with yellow robes and stirred by the wind of saints." So saying he uttered this verse:

"Great is the number of disciples of the Buddha who are arhants, learned in the three kinds of knowledge, gifted with the supernormal powers, skilled in reading the thoughts of others and free from the *āsavas.*"

"Reverend Sir, by what way are you come here?" (And since the answer was:) "Neither by water nor by land, O great king," the king understood that they had come through the air. The thera put a question on the simile of a mango, and the king answered.

Thinking "The king is wise, and will be able to understand the Dhamma," the thera then recited the *Cūlahatthipadopama Sutta.*[1] At the end of the discourse the king with the forty thousand beings came unto the three refuges. "Reverend sir, tomorrow I will send a chariot. Please mount that chariot and come." So saying, the king paid him homage and departed

No sooner had the king departed than the thera ordered the Sāmaṇera Sumana "Sumana, come. Announce the time of hearing the preaching of the Dhamma." "How far, Reverend Sir, shall I make the time to be heard when I announce it?" "Over all the island of Lankā." "It is well, Reverend Sir," replied the Sāmaṇera, and he, entering the fourth stage of meditation, based on apperception, rose up, fixed his attention and

[1] See *Majjhima Nikāya*, I, pp 175-84.

with his mind concentrated and announced thrice the time of hearing the preaching of the Dhamma, making it audible over the whole of the island of Lankā.

When the king heard this sound, he sent a message to the theras (asking): "Reverend Sir, has there been any trouble? There was no trouble for us as we wish to preach the word of the Buddha, we have announced (the time) of hearing the preaching."

When the earth-gods heard the summons of the sāmanera, they echoed it, in this way the call rose up (gradually) to Brahmā's heaven. Because of the summons there came together a great assembly of gods. When the thera had beheld this great assembly of gods, he recited the *Samacitta Suttanta.*[1] At the end of the discourse the gods without number were converted to the doctrine, and many nagas and supaṇṇas came unto the refuges.

When the night had passed, the king sent a chariot for the theras. The charioteer, keeping the chariot on one side, informed the theras "Reverend Sir, the chariot is brought; mount and we will drive (to the city)." "We will not mount the chariot; go thou, we will follow thee." Saying this, the theras rose into the air and descended to the east of Anurādhapura at the place

[1] See *Anguttara-Nikāya*, I, pp 63-65.

where the first cetiya (afterwards stood). And the cetiya, which was built on the spot where the theras first alighted, is called Pathamaka-cetiya the First Shrine. The charioteer saw that the theras had come first, and had fastened girdles and put on robes. As he saw, he was very much gladdened at heart, came and informed the king: "Lord, the theras are come." The king enquired. "Did they mount the chariot?" "They did not, lord. Moreover, they starting after me have come earlier, and are staying at the eastern gate." The king, too, went, paid homage to the theras, took the alms-bowl from the thera Mahinda's hand, and with great honour and homage led the theras into the city and into the palace.

The thera, seeing the immovable seat prepared, and thinking, "the religion of our Teacher will be founded all over the island of Lankā as this immovable seat on the earth," took his seat.

The king himself served the theras with excellent rice-soup and with food hard and soft. The thera having finished the meal, recited the *Petavatthu*, the *Vimānavatthu*, and the *Sacca-saṁyutta* causing the shower of jewels of the Dhamma, so to speak, to the king and his attendants.[1] The five hundred women, hearing the preaching of the doctrine by the thera, attained

[1] See *Saṁyutta-Nikāya*, V, pp. 414-78.

to the first stage of sanctification (*i.e.*, Sotāpatti) At the end of the preaching of the Dhamma, in the evening, the ministers led the theras to the great Meghavana-park The theras stayed in the Meghavana-park. When the night had passed, the king, too, visited the theras and asked about the comfort in their rest. He also asked "Is an *ārāma* allowed to the Order of bhikkhus?" The thera replied: "It is allowed, O great king." The king being pleased, and taking a golden vase, poured water over the hand of the thera and dedicated the great Meghavana-park. As the water fell (on the ground), the earth quaked. For a week the thera preached the Dhamma. Nine thousand five hundred persons were converted The thera went to the Cetiya mountain, and the king also came there.

That very day, a minister named Ariṭṭha with his fifty-five elder and younger brothers, after paying homage to the king, said thus "Lord, I wish to receive the *pabbajjā* from the thera." The king gave him permission (saying) "It must be well said, receive the pabbajjā," and made the thera agree On that same day the thera conferred the *Pabbajjā* All these men attained to Arahantship even in the shaving hall.

To this effect said the Ancients :

13 "When the king, on the same day, had made a beginning with the work of building sixty-

eight rock-cells about (the place where) the Kaṇṭaka-cetiya (afterwards stood),

14 he returned to the city; but the theras remained in that spot, going at the appointed time, full of compassion (for the people), to the city to beg alms there.

15 When the work on the rock-cells was finished, on the full-moon day of the month of Āsāḍha, the king came and gave the vihāra to the theras as a consecrated offering

16 When the thera, who had passed beyond the boundaries (of evil) had established the boundaries for the thirty-two mālakas and the vihāra, then did he, on the very same day,

17 in the Tumbaru-mālaka, which was marked out as the first of all, confer the *upasampadā* on all those who were weary of the *pabbajjā*.

18 And these sixty-two arahants, during the rainy-season, taking up their abode all together on the Cetiya-mountain, showed favour to the king (by their teaching).''[1]

Here ends the chapter, called 'The Acceptance of the Cetiyapabbatavihāra,' in the *Saddhammasaṃgaha*, compiled for the serene joy and emotion of the pious.

[1] See *Mahāvaṃsa*, Ch XVI vv 12-17, for translation see Geiger, *ibid*, p 116

CHAPTER V

THE FOURTH COUNCIL

Thereafter on the day when the relics of the right collar-bone (of the Buddha) were laid down in the Thupārāma, those bhikkhus who coming from the city had received the *Pabbajjā*, numbered thirty thousand in all. Then on the day, when the great Bo-tree was planted, the queen Anulā with five hundred maidens and five hundred women of the harem, thus numbering a thousand of the womenfolk, having received the *Pabbajjā* from the Therī Saṃghamittā, attained, in no time, to arahantship with her retinue. The king's nephew (sister's son) Aitṭha, too, with five hundred men having received the Pabbajjā from the thera, attained to Arahantship shortly

Then the king asked the thera Mahinda[1]: "Is the *Sāsana* established in the island of Lankā, Reverend Sir?" "It is established, O great king; but the roots of the *Sāsana* have not as yet descended." "Reverend sir, when will the roots be called as descended?" "Only when a son, born of the parents inhabiting the island of Lankā, having received the *Pabbajjā* and having acquired the Vinaya in the island of Lankā, recites it, shall

[1] *Cf. Samantapāsādikā*, pp. 341-43.

the roots of the *Sāsana* be called as descended." "Is there, Reverend Sir, such a bhikkhu?" "There is, O great king, a bhikkhu named Arittha the great, who is able in this respect" "In this connection, Reverend Sir, what should be done by me?" "A hall is to be built, O great king."

"It is well," replied the king. And at the place where the parivena built by the minister Meghavannābhaya stood, when he with his royal might had a hall built like that built by the great king Ajātasattu at the time of the Great Council, and had all the musicians engaged to display their respective skill, he thought: "We will see the *Sāsana* descending," and being attended by many thousands of his people reached the Thūpārāma.

At that time one thousand bhikkhus assembled in the Thūpārāma. Facing the south a seat was prepared for the great thera Mahinda. The preacher's seat facing the north was prepared for the great thera Arittha Now, asked by the thera Mahinda, the great thera Arittha, paying homage to the elder bhikkhus, took his proper seat according to his rank Sixty-eight theras, headed by the thera Mahinda, were seated round the preacher's seat The king's younger brother named thera Mantābhaya thought "With utmost endurance I will learn the Vinaya," and he with five hundred bhikkhus remained seated also round the preacher's seat (prepared) for the great thera Ariṭṭha. And the remaining bhikkhus including the king and their attendants were seated in the seats assigned to them.

Then the venerable thera Ariṭṭha the great spoke on the source of the Vinaya. "At that time the Exalted Buddha was staying on (the bank of) the Verañjarā, at the foot of the Nalerupucimanda" And as the source of the Vinaya was spoken by the venerable thera Ariṭṭha, there was a great sound in the sky, flashes of lightning unexpectedly shone forth, gods shouted applause and the great earth encircled by the ocean quaked. Thus when were manifested many wonders, the venerable thera Ariṭṭha, surrounded by the sixty-eight great theras who had each followers and were free from the āsavas, with the thera Mahinda at their head, and by the sixty thousand bhikkhus besides, expounded, on the first great pavāranā-day in the month of Kattika (kārtika), in the monastery of the Thūpārāma, the Vinaya-Piṭaka which brightens the compassion of the Teacher, explains the reason for the Exalted One's admonitions, and removes the scuffling of actions bodily and vocal. Even as the the thera Mahākassapa and the thera Yasa, and the thera Tissa, Moggali's son, had rehearsed the Dhamma and the Vinaya by way of Piṭakas, Nikāyas, Angas, and units of text, so did the great thera Mahinda, while rehearsing the Dhamma and the Vinaya, hold the Fourth Council, making the root of the *Sāsana* descended in the island of Laṅkā. When the council came to a close, the great earth quaked in many ways. This council ended in an indefinite time.

To this effect said the Ancients

19 "When two hundred and thirty-eight years had passed by after the attainment of the Parinibbāna by the Sambhuddha, Piyatissaka became a king

20 Even as the thera Mahākassapa and Yasa, and Tissa had held the Dhamma Council, so also did Mahinda

21 The best doctrine of the Conqueror, the learning (of the Scriptures), its practice and right comprehension did the great thera Mahinda.

22 *Explain in the island of Lankā, and did* he, the great sage of the island of Lankā, who was like the Teacher in Lankā, many welfares to Lankā.

23 The sixty-eight great theras, who having utmost endurance assembled, were all leaders of separate companies, and were the disciples of the King of Righteousness

24 They were free from the āsavas, controlled in their senses, skilled in the three kinds of knowledge and gifted with the supernormal powers, themselves knowing the highest good preached it to the king

25 These great sages, holding the Fourth Council and doing many good to the world, entered into Nibbāna, shining like the columns of fire.

26 Thus knowing that this life is transient and hard to win, be wise and exert yourself for the attainment of the everlasting and immortal state.

Here ends the chapter, called 'The Fourth Council,' in the *Saddhammasamgaha*, compiled for the serene joy and emotion of the pious.

Chapter VI

The Account of the Writing of the Three Piṭakas in Books

After the attainment of the Parinibbāna by those theras, others, such as, Tissa, Danta, Kālasumana, Dīghasumana, and the rest, who were disciples of those theras, as well as the disciples of the great thera Ariṭṭha, having thus formed a succession of teachers as stated above, brought this Vinaya Piṭaka down to the present time

Hence to this effect it has been said.

"After the Third Council (the Vinaya-Piṭaka) was carried to this island of Lankā by Mahinda and others Having learnt from Mahinda, did the thera Ariṭṭha and others carry it for some time. Thereafter it has been carried successively up to the present time by their disciples through a succession of teachers."

Where was it established? It was established among such persons in whom even as oil poured in an ivory pot does not ooze even a little, so was it complete in text and meaning, and who were mindful, of right conduct, resolute, modest, conscientious and anxious for training Thus it should be understood. Therefore, in order to establish the Vinaya Piṭaka, the Vinaya should be mastered by a bhikkhu anxious for training, after considering the advantage of learning it The advantage of learning the Vinaya is this A person expert in the Vinaya-learning deserves the position of parents of the faithful sons of (good) families. This then is utilised by them for their initiation, ordination, accomplishment in all kinds of practices and good behaviour. Besides, because of his Vinaya-learning his own body of morality becomes well guarded and well protected; he protects those bhikkhus who are scrupulous by nature; in the Order, he is known as self-possessed; he reasonably holds backs his opponents to complete suppression. And whatever good deeds based upon self-restraint have been explained by the Exalted One, a person expert in the Vinaya inherits those deeds, for they are based upon the norm of good conduct.

This was also said by the Exalted One

Discipline is for the purpose of restraint, which is for the purpose of absence of remorse, which is for the purpose of gladness, which is for the purpose of rapture, which is for the purpose of repose, which is for the purpose of bliss, which is for the purpose of concentration, which is for the purpose of knowing and seeing the truth, which is for the purpose of disgust, which is for the purpose of dispassion, which is for the purpose of emancipation, which is for the purpose of knowing and seeing emancipation, which is for the purpose of birthless Parinibbāna. For such purpose is the discourse (on the Discipline), for such purpose is the consultation, for such purpose is the groundwork, for such purpose is the attentiveness, namely, the emancipation of the mind devoid of grasping.[1]

Therefore one should exert for the Vinaya-learning

To this effect has it been said ·

1 "The king Devānampiyatissa, lord of Lankā, virtuous and wise, reigned forty years

2 After his death, his younger brother, known as Uttiya, became ruler and ruled in splendid Anurādhapura.

3 Mahānāga, the Vice-regent, Yatāla of great might, Gothābhaya of great merit, and Kākavanna the energetic

4 These four kings as (his) sons and grandsons, reigned successively with piety in pleasant Mahāgāma."

Three hundred seventy-six years after the attainment of the Parinibbāna by the Exalted One, the great king Dutthagāmini-abhaya gained sovereignty over the island of Lankā When he had built the Maricavatti-vihāra, he made the Lohapāsāda nine-storied When he had completed the Great Thūpa overlaid with gem-dusts, he assembled the bhikkhus among whom the arahants were ninety-six kotis, and bestowed (on them) a

[1] Cf Visuddhimagga, Vol I

great gift. When he had reigned piously and justly twenty-four years in Anurādhapura he was reborn, as one awakened from sleep, in the Tusita heaven at the expiry of his life term. At that time, the Order of bhikkhus residing in the island of Lankā mastered the entire saying of the Buddha, comprised in the three Pitakas, with text and the commentary thereon, which for the growth of the *Sāsana* was orally handed down through a succession (of teachers).

To this effect said the Ancients

5 "When two hundred seventy-six years had passed since the attainment of the Parinibbāna by the Sambuddha, Dutthagāmini became king.

6 Dutthagāmini-abhaya, lord of Lankā, virtuous and wise, reigned in Lankā twenty-four years.

7 Thus the lord of the earth, doing many meritorious deeds, was, after the dissolution of his body, reborn with knowledge in the Tusita heaven."

[The story of the birth of great king Dutthagāmini-abhaya.]

When fifty-seven years had passed since the founding of the Great Thūpa, the great King Vattagāmini-abhaya reigned in the island of Lankā. When this king had built a great vihāra at the Abhayagiri, he erected in that vihāra a great Cetiya to the extent of the Great Thūpa, with a relic (chamber), and dedicated it to the Order of bhikkhus headed by the Thera Mahātissa

At that time the Order of bhikkhus residing in the island of Laṅkā realised that there would be the decline of the *Sāsana* and of the people, and in the Mahāvihāra came together all the bhikkhus who were expert in the Dhamma, expert in the Vinaya, learned, and advanced in analytic insight. Then the great king Vattagāmini-abhaya went to the Mahāvihāra and approached the Order of bhikkhus. Having approached, he paid homage to the Order of bhikkhus and took his seat on one side. Then the Order of bhikkhus said to the king: "O great king, the entire saying of the Buddha comprised in the three Pitakas, with text and the commentary thereon, which was orally handed down through a succession (of teachers) has been even now handed down orally. In future, there will be the decline of the *Sāsana* and of the people and the entire saying of the Buddha, comprised in the three Pitakas, with text and the commentary thereon, will be lost. Therefore the entire saying of the Buddha, comprised in the three Pitakas, with text and the commentary thereon, should now be written down in books" "Reverend Sir, what should be done by me in this matter?" "A hall should be built and all the leaves should be provided for the books, O great king." "It is well, Reverend Sir," replied the king. And in the Mahāvihāra when he with his royal might had a hall built like that built by the great king Ajātasattu at the time of the Great Council, and had all the leaves provided for books, he caused highly precious seats to be laid down in the middle of the hall, and bade his people inform the Order of bhikkhus: "My work is finished, Reverend Sir."

Then out of bhikkhus who were many hundred thousands in number, the Order of bhikkhus chose many thousand elder bhikkhus, expert in the learning of the three Piṭakas, advanced in analytic insight, able to refute the threefold knowledge (of the Vedas), and the like. Then the elder bhikkhus took their respective seats assigned to them. Even as the thera Mahākassapa and the thera Yasa, and the thera Tissa, and the thera Mahinda while rehearsing the Dhamma and the Vinaya had rehearsed them by way of Piṭakas, Nikāyas, Angas, and units of text, so did the Order of bhikkhus, while causing the Dhamma and the Vinaya to be written down in books from what had been orally handed down, cause the Buddha's saying, comprised in the three Piṭakas and known as the Dhamma and the Vinaya, with text and the commentary thereon, to be written down in books, and hold it as the Fifth Council enabling the *Sāsana* to endure a period of five thousand years. When the writing of the Dhamma was completed, the great earth quaked in many ways. This writing of the three Piṭakas was completed in one year.

To this effect said the Ancients:[1]

8 When four hundred and thirty-three years had passed since the attainment of the Parinibbāna by the Sambuddha, Vaṭṭagāmini became king.

9 The Order of bhikkhus who resided in Laṅkā looking at the future, found that there would be the falling away of beings, and the bhikkhus then came together

10 All of them were expert in the three Piṭakas, advanced in analytic insight, free from the āsavas, self-controlled, and highly skilled in the Vinaya.

11 In that Mahāvihāra, the elder bhikkhus assembled and took their respective seats assigned to them according to their ranks

12 The text of the three Piṭakas and the commentary thereon did the most wise bhikkhus hand down orally in former times

13 As recited in the Councils, all the three Piṭakas did these theras rehearse together with the commentary thereon.

14 In order that the doctrine might endure long and the *Sāsana* might prosper, (they were) made capable of lasting a period of five thousand years

15 The entire Vinaya as recited did the theras, skilled in the Vinaya, cause to be written down in books

[1] *Cf Dīpavaṃsa*, Ch XX, 20 21, for verses 12, 21, see *Mahāvaṃsa*, Ch XXXIII, vv 100, 102

16 The entire Sutta-Piṭaka as recited did the theras, skilled in the Suttanta, cause to be written down in books.

17 And the Abhidhamma-Piṭaka as recited did the theras, skilled in the Abhidhamma, cause to be written down in books.

18 The entire Theravāda and the entire commentary thereon did they hand down orally and cause them to be written down in books.

19 When the writing was completed, the great earth quaked, and various wonders manifested themselves in many ways in this world.

20 All these theras having written down the three Piṭakas and doing many good to the world, lived their allotted span of life and entered into Nibbāna.

21 Thus did Vaṭṭagāmini-abhaya reign in Lankā twelve years, and, at the beginning, five months

22 Thus the lord of earth doing many meritorious deeds, was, after the dissolution of his body, reborn in heaven with knowledge.

23 Thus knowing that life is transient and hard to win, be wise and exert yourself to attain the everlasting and immortal state

Here ends the Chapter, called 'The Account of the Writing of the Three Piṭakas in Books,' in the *Saddhammasaṃgaha*, compiled for the serene joy and emotion of the pious

CHAPTER VII

The Account of the Translation of the Atthakatha of the Three Pitakas

Five hundred and sixteen years after the writing of the three Piṭakas, a king named Mahānāma reigned in the island of Lankā. At that time, a young brāhmana was born in a brāhmana family in the neighbourhood of the Bo-terrace in the Middle country in Jambudīpa. Skilled in all the sciences and versed in the three Vedas, he wandered through villages, towns, countries, and cities in Jambudīpa, and wherever learned men, samanas, and brāhmanas, lived, he would visit those places and discuss (with them). Questions asked by him, others were not able to explain, but he would answer questions put by others. Thus going all around Jambudīpa, he came to a vihāra In that vihāra lived many hundred bhikkhus. The senior of the Order of those bhikkhus was a venerable thera named Revata, the foremost of those who were free from āsavas, possessed of analytical insight, and capable of crushing the views of their opponents. Now, the young brāhmana repeating a hymn day and night, became perfect in all its component parts. Then the thera listened to the recitation of the brāhmana, and thought thus : "This brāhmana is of profound knowledge. It behoves me to convert him." Then (the thera) addressing him, said thus "O brāhmana. who is this who is braying like an ass?" The brāhmaṇa replied: "O Recluse, you know not then the meaning conveyed in the bray of an ass." When (the thera) rejoined "Yes, I know." The brāhmana asked the thera regarding all knotty points, found in the three Vedas and in the fifth (branch of brāhmanical learning, namely,) the Itihāsa, the sense of which neither he would find nor did his teacher realise As usual, the thera became versed in the three Vedas, but then as he was possessed of analytical insight, it was not a difficult thing for him to answer those questions, and when he had answered those questions then and there, he asked the brāhmana: "O brāhmana, many questions I have been asked by you, let me also now ask you only one question, (I think) you will answer it." "Yes, Recluse, ask, I will answer." From the *Cittayamaka*[1] the thera asked this question:

"A unit of consciousness which functions, and has not yet disappeared, will that unit of consciousness disappear, will that unit not function? Or else, a unit of consciousness which will disappear, will not function, will that unit of consciousness function, will that unit not disappear?" The brāhmaṇa, unable to make out its

[1] Comprised in the *Yamaka* (Section VIII) of the Abhidhammapitaka.

meaning asked: "What is this, Recluse?" "Brāhmaṇa, it is the Buddha's *manta*" "Can you impart it to me?" "O Brāhmana, we can impart it to him who on receiving ordination wants to take it." Then the brāhmana asked for ordination for the sake of the *manta*. The thera ordained him and admitted him into the Order. The thera then taught him the whole of the Buddha's saying, comprised in the three Piṭakas.

To this effect said the Ancients[1]:

1 "A brāhmana youth was born in the neighbourhood of the terrace of the great Bo-tree, who was accomplished in the 'vijjā' and 'sippa,' and versed in the three Vedas.

2 Possessed of great aptitude in attaining acquirements, indefatigable as a schismatic disputant, and himself a schismatic wanderer over Jambudīpa, he established himself in the character of a disputant.

3 He came to a certain vihāra, and was in the habit of rehearsing, by night and by day, with clasped hands, a discourse which he had learnt perfectly in all its component parts, and sustained throughout in the same lofty strain

4 A certain mahāthera, Revata, becoming acquainted with him there, thought "This individual is a person of profound knowledge; it will be worthy (of me) to convert him."

[1] *Mahāvamsa* (Turnour ed), pp 250-251 Verses 9-10 show a somewhat different reading in the text

5 He enquired: "Who is this who is braying like an ass?" (The brāhmaṇa) replied to him: "Thou canst define, then, the meaning conveyed in the bray of asses."

6 On (the thera) rejoining: "I can define it," (the brāhmaṇa) exhibited the extent of the knowledge he possessed. (The thera) answered each of his propositions and pointed out in what respect they were fallacious.

7 Being refuted, he said "Well then, descend to thy own creed." And the thera explained to him a passage from the Abhidhamma (The brāhmaṇa) could not divine the meaning of that (passage)

8 (The brāhmana) enquired: "Whose *manta* is this?" (The thera) replied: "It is the Buddha's *manta*." On (the former's) exclaiming "Impart it to me," (the latter replied:) "Take ordination."

9 He who had been refuted on the aforesaid grounds obtained ordination for the sake of the *manta*. The thera ordained him and taught him the *Kammatthānas* (grounds for contemplation).

10 Having been ordained he learned the three Pitakas, and became as renowned as the sun or the moon.

11 As he was as profound in his eloquence (*ghosa*) as the Buddha himself, (they) conferred on him the appellation of Buddhaghosa, (*i e.*, the

voice of the Buddha); and throughout the world Ghosa became as renowned as the Buddha.

Thenceforward throughout the world this bhikkhu, known as the Thera Buddhaghosa, became renowned. Then in that vihāra, he composed an original work called the *Ñānodaya*. He also wrote a commentary on the Dhammasangaṇi, called the *Atthasālinī*, and then he commenced to compile a *Parittaṭṭhakathā* (*i.e*, a general commentary on the three Pitakas). Then the venerable Thera Revata seeing this, said thus "Friend Buddhaghosa, here in Jambudīpa, the text alone of the three Pitakas has been preserved, the commentary thereon and the opinions of teachers (*ācariyavādā*) are not extant here. But the Sinhalese commentaries, composed in the Sinhalese language by Mahinda who had previously consulted the account given by Sāriputta and others, and authenticated at the three councils, are extant in the island of Sīhala Repairing thither, and examining the same, translate (them) into the dialect of Magadha It will be an act conducive to the welfare of the whole world

Having been thus advised, Buddhaghosa became glad and satisfied, and when he, paying homage to his preceptor and the Order of bhikkhus, had obtained their permission, he on his way reached Nāgapaṭṭana Then Sakka, king of the gods, offered him a myrobalan fruit and a pen, and departed to his own abode Then Buddhaghosa boarded a ship, and on his way he met the venerable Thera Buddhadatta on the great ocean and held conversation with him Thereafter he reached Lankāpattana, in the reign of this king Mahānāma When he had visited the Order of bhikkhus in the Mahāvihāra in Anurādhapura, and approached the Thera Samghapāla in the Mahāpadhāna Hall, he listened to the entire Sinhalese commentary and the Theravāda, and became convinced "This conveys the true meaning of the doctrine of the Buddha; lord of Dhamma." And in that vihāra having assembled the Order, he petitioned thus. Reverend members of the Order, I wish to translate the commentaries, give me access to all your books"

Then the Order of bhikkhus, for the purpose of testing his qualifications, gave only two stanzas, saying. "Having satisfied ourselves with thy qualifications, we will let thee have all our books" Then the venerable Buddhaghosa consulting the text of the three Pitakas and the commentary thereon, compiled a book called the *Visuddhimagga*. Thereupon the gods in order to make the gift of his wisdom known among the multitude, rendered that book invisible. He recomposed a second copy, and this, too, did the gods make invisible He recomposed for the third time. At that moment the gods restored the other two copies also. There were then three copies.

Thereupon the venerable Buddhaghosa taking the three copies, presented them to the Order of bhikkhus. The order of bhikkhus then read out the three copies simultaneously. In those three copies, neither in composition nor in syllables, nor in words, nor in letters, nor in sense, not in arrangement, nay, even in the Theravāda tradition and the like, and also in the test, was there the slightest variation.

To this effect said the Ancients [1]

12 "Then having there (in Jambudīpa) compiled an original work called the *Ñānodaya*, he wrote the *Atthasālinī*, a commentary on the Dhammasangani.

13 The wise then commenced to compile a *Parittaṭṭhakathā*, and the Thera Revata seeing it, said in these words:

14 "The text alone (of the three Piṭakas) has been preserved in this land The Aṭṭhakathās are not extant here; nor is there the Theravāda or any other version to be found.

15 & 16 The Sinhalese Aṭṭhakathā are genuine. They were composed in the Sinhalese language by the profoundly wise Mahinda with due regard to the methods of exposition as taught by the Buddha, put up before the three councils, and rehearsed by Sāriputta and others, and they are extant among the people of Simhala.

17 Repairing thither and listening to the same, translate (them) into the dialect of Magadha.

[1] *Mahāvamsa* (Turnour ed), pp 251-252

It will be an act conducive to the welfare of the whole world."

18 Having been thus advised, this profoundly wise person rejoicing therein, departed from there and visited this island (of Lankā) in the reign of this king (Mahānāma).

19 On reaching the Mahāvihāra, the most splendid of all vihāras, he entered the Mahāpadhāna Hall and approached Saṃghapāla.

20 He listened there to the Sinhalese Aṭṭhakathā and the Theravāda, all complete, and was convinced: 'This conveys the true meaning of the doctrines of the Lord of Dhamma.'

21 Having assembled the Order there, he petitioned 'I wish to translate the Atthakathās; give me access to all your books.' For the purpose of testing his qualifications.

22 The Order gave him only two gāthās, saying 'Hence prove thy qualification; having satisfied ourselves on this point, we will then let thee have all our books.'

23 From these (two gāthās) he, consulting the three Piṭakas and the Aṭṭhakathā thereon and condensing them into an abridged form, composed a book called the *Visuddhimagga*.

24 Thereupon having assembled the Order who had acquired a thorough knowledge of the doctrines of the Buddha, at the Bo-tree, he commenced to read out (his composition).

25 The devatās in order to make the gift of his wisdom celebrated among men, rendered that book invisible He, too, recomposed it for the third time

26 When he was in the act of producing his book for the third time, for the purpose of expounding it, the devatās restored the other two copies also.

27 The (assembled) bhikkhus then read out the three books simultaneously. Neither in sound, nor in significance, nor in arrangement,

28 nay even in the theravāda and in the text was there, in the measure of verses, or in letters, the slightest variation in those three versions."

When the three copies of the book had been prepared, a great sound was heard, untimely thunders clapped, and the gods shouted applause in the air. At that time many thousand bhikkhus who had come together in the Mahāvihāra, saw that wonder, and being pleased and gladdened, they gave applause, and shouted again and again, saying : "Most assuredly this is Metteyya Bodhisatta." Then on hearing this, king Mahānāma, attended by a great royal party, came out of the city and went to the Mahāvihāra. Paying homage to the Order of bhikkhus, he invited the venerable thera Buddhaghosa after showing due honour to him. "Reverend Sir, please take thy meal in my palace until the preaching of the doctrines is finished." He consented silently.

Then the Order of bhikkhus gave him the books in which the text of the three Piṭakas was recorded together with the books of the Sinhalese commentaries Then did the venerable Buddhaghosa take all those books, and while dwelling in a mansion called the Padhānaghara on the southern side of the Mahāvihāra, he translated all the Sinhalese commentaries, and rendered the commentaries on the three Piṭakas into the dialect of Magadha, which is the basic language

In the *Samanta-pāsādikā*, three kinds of commentaries are spoken of What are they? (They are) : *Mahā-aṭṭhakathā*, *Mahā-paccari-aṭṭhakathā*, and *Mahā-kurunda-aṭṭhakathā*. These three kinds of commentaries constitute the Sinhalese Aṭṭhakathā. The Mahā-Aṭṭhakathā was so called because having been made by the theras with Mahākassapa at their head, and authenticated in First Great Council, it was brought over and translated into the Sinhalese language by the great Mahinda. In the Sinhalese language, it is said, there was a raft (*paccari*); hence sitting there the Aṭṭhakathā, which was compiled, came to be known as the great 'Raft' commentary (*Mahā-paccarī*). There was the Kurundavelu-vihāra (in Lankā); hence sitting there the Aṭṭhakathā, which was composed, came to be known as Kuruṇḍi commentary.

Then the venerable Buddhaghosa after having translated the Sinhalese Kurunda-Atthakathā into the dialect of Magadha which is the basic language, compiled a commentary on the Vinaya-Piṭaka, called the *Samanta-pāsādikā*

As to this, it is said :

29 "Skilled in the Vinaya, he, for the growth of the *Sāsana*, undertook the compilation of a commentary on the Vinaya in the dialect of Magadha

30 And he completed all round his work called the *Samanta-pāsādikā*, extending up to twenty-seven thousand syllables."

Then in the Sutta-Piṭaka, after having translated the Sinhalese Mahā-Atthakathā, he compiled a commentary on the Dīgha-Nikāya, called the *Sumangalavilāsinī*. So also he compiled a commentary on the Majjhima-Nikāya, called the *Papañcasūdanī* Similarly he compiled a commentary on the Samyutta-Nikāya, called the *Sāratthappakāsinī*. Likewise, he compiled a commentary on the Anguttara-Nikāya, called the *Manorathapūraṇī*.

As to this, it is said

31 "Skilled in the Suttanta, he for the growth of the *Sāsana*, undertook the compilation of the commentaries on the Suttanta.

32 And he completed, all round the commentaries on the four Nikāyas, extending up to eighty thousand syllables.

33 He also completed, all round a commentary on the Khuddaka-Nikāya, extending up to thirty-seven thousand syllables."

Thereafter in the Abhidhamma-Pitaka, he, after having translated the Sinhalese Mahāpaccari-Aṭṭhakathā into the dialect of Magadha, which is the basic language, compiled a commentary on the Dhammasangani, called the *Atthasālinī*. So he compiled a commentary, called the *Sammoha-vinodanī*, on a book entitled the Vibhaṅga.

As to this it has been said

34 "Skilled in the Abhidhamma, he, for the growth of the *Sāsana*, undertook the compilation of the commentaries on the Abhidhamma in the dialect of Magadha.

35 He completed all round (these commentaries), called the *Atthasālinī* and the like, extending up to thirty thousand syllables."

And in the dialect of Magadha, he rendered the Aṭṭhakathā on the entire Theravāda, adopted in former times by the adherents of the Theravāda, the Ācariyavāda, and the like, with due regard to the method of the text. This compilation of the Aṭṭhakathā on the Piṭakas was an act conducive to the welfare of the inhabitants of all countries. When the Aṭṭhakathā on the Pitakas was completed, the great earth quaked in many ways The writing of this Aṭṭhakathā on the Piṭakas was completed in one year.

Then the venerable Buddhaghosa, having finished his task, wished to worship the great Bo-tree, and he, paying homage to the Order of bhikkhus and taking their permission, returned to Jambudīpa

To this effect said the Ancients[1] :

36 "When nine hundred and fifty-six years had passed since the attainment of the Parinibbāna by the Sambuddha, Mahānāma, lord of men, reigned in Lankā with ten kinds of piety.

37 As he was as profound in his eloquence as the Buddha himself, throughout the world Ghosa became as renowned as the Buddha. He came to the island of Lankā, and proved himself of its utmost benefit

38 The Order gave (him) only two verses and the Sinhalese commentary, and he, with the permission of the Order, compiled the *Visuddhimagga*.

39 Then the Order, being exceedingly pleased and gladdened, shouted again and again, saying. 'Most assuredly this is Metteya (Bodhisatta).'

40 The Order gave (him) the books of the three Pitakas together with the commentary thereon He took up his residence in the secluded Ganthākāra (vihāra).

41 The whole of the Sinhalese Aṭṭhakathā did he then translate into the dialect of Magadha, which is the root of all languages.

[1] For verses 39-41, see *Mahāvaṃsa* (Turnour ed.), pp. 252-253.

42 This proved an achievement of the utmost consequence to all languages spoken by the human race All the theras and ācariyas held this compilation in the same estimation as the text (of the canon).

43 Thereafter, his task having been finished he returned to Jambudīpa to worship the great Bo-tree

44 Mahānāma, having enjoyed the great earth twenty-two years, and doing many meritorious deeds, departed accordingly.

45 And the thera, having compiled the Atthakathā on the Pitakas and doing many good to the world, lived his allotted span of life and was reborn in the Tusita heaven.

46 The elder bhikkhus, dwellers of Lanka who had their task done, and were free from the āsavas, then lived their alloted span of life and all of them also entered into Nibbāna "

47 Thus knowing that life is transient and hard to win, be wise and exert yourself to attain the everlasting and immortal state

Here ends the Chapter, called 'The Account of the Translation of the Atthakathā of the Three Piṭakas' in the *Saddhammasamgaha*, compiled for the serene joy and emotion of the pious.

CHAPTER VIII

The Account of the Ṭikas of the Three Piṭakas

Thereafter when six hundred and eighty-three years had passed since the translation of the commentaries on the three Piṭakas, a great king named Parakkamabāhu, following the line of Mahāsammata, was born in the Solar-race. After his father's death when he had defeated the hostile kings of three kingdoms, he was consecrated as a universal monarch of the whole of Laṅkā and he, as a paramount sovereign shining forth with his glory that spread throughout his country and elsewhere, reigned righteously in the great city of Pulatthī When he had found that the *Sāsana*, divided into different sects, having been decayed after one thousand one hundred and fifty-four years from the time of the great king Vaṭṭagāmani-abhaya, the *Kulaputtas* (lit. the sons of good families) belonging to the *Sāsana* had shared loss, he, with his heart moved with compassion, thought. "How shall I make the *Sāsana* prosper?" After having completely subdued many hundred wicked bhikkhus, robed them in white garment, turned them out of the Order and purified the *Sāsana*. Under the leadership of thera Mahākassapa King Parakkamabāhu built great vihāras together with the cetiyas at Jetavana, Pubbārāma, DakkhināRāma, Uttarārāma, Veluvana, Kapilavatthu, Isipatana, Kusinārārāma, and Lankātilaka. He also caused an Uposatha Hall to be erected, which was a great mansion with eleven stories and one thousand compartments, decorated with a tower, and rich in paintings and creeper-works. Then he built a great vihāra named Jetavana, adorned with rows of Bo-trees, stūpas, cells, huts and halls, filled with fragrance of flowers of various kinds of best trees, frequented by birds, such as the *kokilas* (cuckoos) and the rest and provided them with tanks full of cool water and covered with *paduma*, *uppala*, and *puṇḍarika* varieties of lotus.

The venerable thera Mahākassapa, who was the senior of the Order of many thousand bhikkhus, assembled the order of bhikkhus there Then the venerable thera Mahākassapa addressed the bhikkhus "Friends, the whole of the Atthavannanā, compiled by the ancients for the purpose of explaining the hidden meaning of the Atthakathā of the three Piṭakas, does not serve the purpose of bhikkhus residing in different countries Some are written in many terse expressions according to the grammar of the Sinhalese language, some are written in the dialect of Magadha, which is the basic language, but they have been confused and twisted by translation. We should, removing the drawback in the translation, compile a complete and clear Atthavaṇṇanā." The bhikkhus replied "Reverend Sir, let the thera get the king issue an order therefor"

At that time the king with his following came out of the city and went to the Vihāra Paying homage to the Order of bhikkhus headed by the thera Mahākassapa, he took his seat on one side.

Then the thera said to him: "O great king, should the compilation of the Atthavannanā of the Aṭṭhakathās of the Pitakas be thy duty" "It is well, reverend sir, I will lend my bodily co-operation; let the Order of bhikkhus be confident." Thereafter the king, paying homage to the Order of bhikkhus, entered the city.

Then the elder bhikkhus, having finished their meal, assembled in the mansion, built by king Parakkamabāhu, and beginning with an Atthavannanā of the Samantapāsādikā, an Atthakathā on the Vinaya-Pitaka, compiled an Atthavannanā, called the *Sāratthadīpanī*, in the dialect of Magadha which is the basic language.

As to this has it been said

1 "For proficiency in the Vinaya and for the growth of the Sāsana, they undertook the compilation of a Vannanā of the Aṭṭhakathā on the Vinaya.

2 They completed all round a work called the *Sāratthadīpanī*, extending up to thirty thousand syllables."

Thereafter beginning with an Atthavannanā of the *Sumangalavilāsinī*, an Atthakathā on the Dīgha Nikāya in the Suttanta-Piṭaka, they compiled an Atthavannanā, called the first *Sāratthamañjusā*, in the dialect of Magadha, which is the basic language. Similarly, beginning with an Atthavaṇṇanā of the Papañcasūdanī, an Aṭṭhakathā on the Majjhima Nikāya, they compiled an Atthavannanā, called the second *Sāratthamañjusā*, in the dialect of Magadha, which is the basic language. Likewise, beginning with an Atthavannanā of the Sāratthappakāsinī, an Aṭṭhakathā on the Saṃyutta-Nikāya, they compiled an Atthavaṇṇanā called the third *Sāratthamañjusā*, in the dialect of Magadha, which is the basic language. So also, beginning with an Atthavaṇṇanā of the Manorathapūranī, an Aṭṭhakathā on the Aṅguttara-Nikāya, they compiled an Atthavaṇṇanā, called the fourth *Sāratthamañjusā*, in the dialect of Magadha, which is the basic language.

As to this it is said

3 "Skilled in the Suttanta, they, for the growth of the Sāsana, undertook the compilation of a Vannanā of the Aṭṭhakathā on the Suttanta

4 They completed all round a work called the *Sāratthamañjusā*, extending up to ninety-four thousand syllables."

Thereafter beginning with an Atthavannanā of the Atthasālinī, an Atthakathā on the Dhammasangaṇi in the Abhidhamma-Piṭaka, they compiled an original Ṭīkā and a sub-Tīkā, called the first *Paramatthapakāsinī*, in the dialect of Magadha, which is the basic language. Similarly, beginning with an Atthavannanā of the Sammoha-vinodanī, an Aṭṭhakathā on the book called Vibhanga, they compiled an original Ṭīkā and a sub-Tīkā, called the second *Paramatthapakāsinī*, in the dialect of Magadha, which is the basic language Likewise, beginning with an Atthavannanā of the Paramattha-dīpanī, an Atthakathā on the five books (of the Abhidhamma), they compiled an original Ṭīkā and a sub-Ṭīkā called the third *Paramatthapakāsinī*, in the dialect of Magadha, which is the basic language.

To this effect said the Ancients

5 "Skilled in the Abhidhamma, they, for the growth of the Sāsana, undertook the compilation of a Vannanā of the Aṭthakathā on the Abhidhamma.

6 They completed all round the *Paramattha-pakāsinī* extending up to twenty-seven thousand syllables."

Thus being requested by king Parakkama-bāhu, the thera Mahākassapa together with many thousand theras put forth their exertion and even as the rehearsal of the Dhamma and the Vinaya, completed the Atthavaṇṇanā of the Aṭṭhakathā on the Piṭakas. When the compilation of the Attha-vaṇṇanā was completed, many wonders, including the earthquake and the like, were manifested, and the gods shouted applause. This compilation of the

Atthavaṇṇanā of the Atthakathā on the Pitakas was completed in one year.

To this effect said the Ancients:

7 " One thousand five hundred and eighty-seven years after the attainment of the Parinibbāna by the Sambuddha, Parakkama became king

8 He, who was consecrated and fond of the lustre of the Sāsana, suppressed his enemies by the power of his great merit.

9 For this purpose Parakkamabāhu, king of Siṃhala, made the Nikāyas harmonious and the Sāsana pure

10 & 11 Being requested by king Parakkama bāhu who wished that the Sāsana might endure, the great thera Kassapa, leader of the Order, exerted for the Sasana so that the Sāsana might prosper in the island of Tambapaṇṇi.'

12 The explanation of hidden meaning of the Aṭṭhakathā on the Pitakas does not serve altogether the purpose of bhikkhus everywhere.

13 Some are written in many terse expressions according to the Sinhalese grammar which by its nature is difficult to be understood.

14 Some, having made an attempt in the language of Magadha, have written something intermixed with translation.

15 Here, in many places is found the worthlessness in composition; things are not clearly described and they are not intelligible without difficulty in meaning.

16 From what is thus incomplete, how can the inhabitants of different countries make out the meaning throughout

17 From this, leaving aside the translation and taking the substance throughout, I shall make a clear and full exposition.'

18 & 19 The works called the *Sāratthadīpanī*, the *Sāratthamañjusā*, and the *Paramatthappakāsinī*, were expounded by the great theras as Vaṇṇanā of the three Pitakas and as explanation of their hidden meanings. This act was conducive to the welfare of beings and of all languages.

20 The king of Lankā, named Parakkamabhuja, who was pious and wise, reigned in Lankā with ten kinds of piety.

21 He who was a believer in the Three Jewels, doing many meritorious deeds, departed accordingly at the end of his life

22 When the theras, such as Kassapa and others, had compiled the Ṭīkā of the Piṭakas, they also lived their allotted span of life and departed according to their deeds

23 Thus knowing that life is transient and hard to win, be wise and exert yourselves to attain the everlasting and immortal state.

Here ends the Chapter, called 'The Account of the Ṭikās of the Three Pitakas' in the *Saddhammasamgaha*, compiled for the serene joy and emotion of the pious.

CHAPTER IX

The Account of All the Books Compiled by the Theras

1 The text of the three Piṭakas delivered by the Perfectly Enlightened One, contains one thousand one hundred and eighty-three chapters

2 And according to the number of syllables, the text of the three Pitakas contains two lac two nahuta five thousand seven hundred and fifty syllables in number.

3 And according to letters, the text of the three Pitakas contains ninety-four lac and sixty-four thousand letters.

4 The whole Atthakathā of the Pitakas, which was expounded by Buddhaghosa, contains one thousand one hundred and sixty-three chapters.

5 And according to the number of syllables, the whole Atthakathā of the Pitakas contains two lac nine nahuta five thousand seven hundred and fifty syllables.

6 And according to letters, the whole Atthakathā of the Piṭakas contains ninety-three lac and four thousand letters.

7 The Ṭīkā of the three Piṭakas, which was expounded by the teachers of the Ṭīkā, contains,

according to the number of chapters, six hundred and thirty-two chapters.

8 And according to syllables, the Ṭīkā of the three Piṭakas contains one hundred and fifty-eight thousand syllables

9 And according to letters, the Ṭīkā of the three Piṭakas contains fifty hundred and fifty-six thousand letters.

10 The grand work, known as the *Visuddhimagga*, was compiled by the thera Buddhaghosa as an explanation of the meaning of the Piṭakas.

11 The *Kankhā-vitaranī*, an Aṭṭhakathā on the Pāti-mokkha, was also compiled by the wise thera Buddhaghosa.

12 The *Khuddasikkhā*, with thorough mastery, was compiled by the thera Dhammasiri, who was morally strong, for the use of bhikkhus who were beginners.

13 The excellent work, compiled by the thera Buddhadatta, is widely known as the *Abhidhammāvatāra*.

14 The *Paramatta-vinicchaya* was compiled by the thera Aniruddha in the excellent city of Kāñcipura.

15 The *Abhidhammattha-samgaha* was compiled by a thera, named Anuruddha, for the purpose of explaining the Highest Truth.

16 The *Saccasamkhepa*, adorned with varied method, was compiled by a disciple of the thera Ānanda as an exposition of subtle matters.

17 A work, called the Treatise of *Khema*, was compiled by a wise thera named Khema, in edification of the Highest Truth.

18 Kaccāyana, devoted to contemplation, compiled a work called *Saṃghanandi*; Vimalabodhi and Brahmaputta were the authors of its Tīkā.

19 A work called the *Rupasiddhi* was compiled by the wise thera Buddhappiya, who wished that the True Doctrine might endure.

20 The *Abhidhānappadīpikā* was compiled by the wise thera Moggallāna, who wished that the True Doctrine might endure.

21 The masterly *Jinālankāra* was compiled by a thera named Buddharakkhita, who was adorned with the qualities of the Master.

22 The delightful work *Jinacarita* was compiled by the strong-minded thera called Medhaṅkara.

23 A good Tīkā on the Visuddhimagga, which is known as the *Paramatthamañjusā*, was compiled by the wise thera Dhammapāla

24 The book called the *Vinayasamgaha* was compiled by a thera named Sagaramati, revealing the meaning of the Vinaya.

25 A good Vaṇṇanā of the Saccasamkhepa, which is known as the *Nissayatthakathā*, was compiled by a thera named Mahābodhi.

26 A good Vaṇṇanā of the Paramatthavinicchaya, which is known as the *Mukhamattakā*, was compiled by a thera named Mahābodhi.

27 The good *Paramattha-dīpanī*, a Vaṇṇanā of the Vimāna and the Petavatthu, was compiled by the thera Dhammapāla.

28 & 29 The *Subodhālaṃkāra*, the clear *Vuttodaya* and *a Tīkā on the Khuddasikkhā* having been compiled, the *Sambuddha-vaṇṇanā* was compiled by a thera named Saṃgharakkhita, who wished that the True Doctrine might endure and the Sāsana might prosper.

30 The good *Vinayavinicchaya* was compiled by the thera Buddhasīha for the growth of the Sāsana.

31 A good and well-written *Ṭikā on the Kaṅkhā-vitaraṇī* was compiled by a strong-minded thera named Buddhanāga.

32 The beautiful *Paramatthadīpanī*, an Aṭṭhakathā on the Therīgāthā, was compiled by the thera Dhammapāla

33 A good *Ṭīkā on the Abhidhammattha-saṃgaha* was compiled by a wise thera who was a disciple of the thera Sāriputta.

34 And the Dhammapada Atthakathā, with clever references, was compiled by (one) thera Buddhaghosa.

35 The excellent work, known as the *Netti-pakaraṇa*, was compiled by the thera Kaccāyana at the instance of the Enlightened One.

36 A good Vannanā of the Saccasaṃkhepa, known as the *Săratthasālinī*, was compiled by a thera who was a disciple of Sāriputta.

37 Many small and beautiful works were compiled by that thera's disciple who was fond of the lustre of the Sāsana.

38 For the growth of the Sāsana of the Conqueror, all these works were compiled by the theras in adaptation of the three Piṭakas

39 All (these) theras of great might, doing very many good to the world, lived their allotted span of life and then departed according to their deeds.

40 Thus knowing that life is transient and hard to win, be wise and exert yourself to attain the everlasting and immortal state.

Here ends the chapter, called 'The Account of All the Books, Compiled by the Theras' in the *Saddhamma-samgaha*, compiled for the serene joy and emotion of the pious.

CHAPTER X

The Account of the Advantages of Writing the Three Pitakas

Thereafter an account of the advantages of copying the three Pitakas should be related Moreover, the Exalted One lying on the bed of his Parinibbāna, addressed the thera Ānanda, and said:

"Ānanda, the Doctrine and the Discipline which I have set forth and laid down for you all, let them, after I am gone, be the Teacher unto you."[1] "There are eighty-four thousand units of text propounded by me during forty-five years from the time of my Enlightenment up to the attainment of the Parinibbāna. I am to go alone, now I alone instruct and admonish you, but, after I am gone, these eighty-four thousand units of text, like eighty-four thousand Buddhas,[1] will instruct and admonish you"

Thus he formulated eighty-four thousand excellent units of Dhamma, called his own body of Norm, which by themselves had taken the place of the Teacher, as eighty-four thousand excellent self-born Buddhas.

This has been said by the Exalted One.

1 Each letter (in the Piṭakas) should be considered as equal to a Buddha-representation.

[1] See *Mahāparinibbāna-Sutta* (Ch. VI) of the *Digha Nikāya*, Vol II.

Therefore, a wise man should write down the three Piṭakas.

2 If the three Piṭakas last, the Sambuddhas to the extent of eighty-four thousand will also last.

3 Each letter in the Buddha's teaching (contained) in the Scriptures should be considered as having merit equal to a Buddha-representation.

4 Therefore a wise man, who wishes for the threefold wealth, should write it down, or cause it to be written down in a book, or in a memorial in honour of the Dhamma.

5 He who writes down the Dhamma, known as the three Piṭakas, fulfils the ten items of meritorious deeds and the threefold right conduct.

6 He also fulfils thoroughly the Good Norm in three ways, namely, in knowledge, in practice, and in realisation of the teaching.

7 Each letter in the teaching of the Lord of the world should be considered as having merit equal to a Buddha-representation.

8 Therefore a wise man who wishes for the threefold wealth, should write down a letter of the three Pitakas, or cause it to be written down.

9 All the three Piṭakas comprise four hundred crore and seventy-two letters.

10 Those, who write down the Pitakas, do like the making of four hundred crore and seventy-two images (of the Buddha).

The advantage of writing the three Piṭakas should be related by quoting here the advantage of making an image which, in praise of an image in Kośala, the Exalted One declared in detail :

11 "Those, who write down a letter of the three Piṭakas like the making of an image of the Teacher, are reborn in all the worlds with charming bodies and with radiance as the sun.

12 Those who cause a letter of the Piṭaka to be written down, do not undergo their existence either as women or as eunuchs, and the like, having the characteristics of both sexes, but they are born perfect throughout.

13 Those who cause a letter of the Piṭaka to be written down, do not even suffer death by accident, or by a poisonous weapon, or by the *mantras*, and the like, or by the enemy kings, (for) they are led by kindness.

14 Those who cause a letter of the Piṭaka to be written down, are reborn with the most excellent beauty either in a noble Brāhmaṇa family, or in a famous Khattiya family, but they are not born in an inferior or a low family.

15 Those who cause a letter of the Piṭakas to be written down, do not undergo their existence as Petas in the world hereafter, nor are they born dumb, paralysed, blind or deaf. They are set free from the four purgatories.

16 Those who cause a letter of the Piṭaka to be written down, do not suffer in the womb, or even at the time of their birth. Even the mothers who give birth to them, do not suffer.

17 Those who cause a letter of the Pitaka to be written down, prosper yet always in happiness, wealth, enjoyment, fame and the rest, nay, even in all the respects, they grow

18 Those who cause a letter of the Piṭaka to be written down, are not besmeared with dirt, phlegm, and the like, when they are born in the womb, but they remain pure like precious stones on a clean garment

19 Those who cause a letter of the Pitaka to be written down, grow even happily in the womb, and when they come out of their mothers' wombs, they descend even as from the preacher's chair.

20 Those who cause a letter of the Pitaka to be written down, are honoured, like the thousand-eyed (Sakka), with ambrosia (by the gods). Likewise, they, honoured by the chief kings, became the excellent and sovereign kings.

21 Those men who cause a letter of the Dhamma to be written down, if they, after having given up their existence as men, come back to life as gods, obtain the excellent and beautiful celestial abodes.

22 Those who write down a letter of the three Pitakas, rejoice exceedingly (always) and everywhere, (entertained) by the excellent heavenly music of the lovely women, and they feel the highest happiness for a long time.

23 Those who cause a letter of the Piṭaka to be written down, reach the highest state in the

highest deva-world, if they so desire, when they, at the completion of their existence, fall away therefrom.

24 Having obtained the Sambuddhahood which, in the three existences, is the only essential object, the Enlightenment by oneself, and the state of a disciple of great might, they gain the highest bliss of nibbāna.

25 The givers of book-band, clothing, bowl, pen-holder, 'thread for sewing,' or soot, become possessed of the highest wisdom.

26 Those who themselves write, those who make others to write, and those who approve of it, will be, in future, the wise disciples of Metteyya, the Conqueror.

27 Whatever is wished for, prayed for, or delighted in, those who write or pay others (for writing), will gain all at ease in future."[1]

Here ends the Chapter, called the 'Account of the Advantages of Writing the Three Piṭakas' in the *Saddhammasaṃgaha*, compiled for the serene joy and emotion of the pious.

[1] The source can not be traced

CHAPTER XI

The Account of the Advantages of Hearing the Preaching of the Norm

Thereafter an account of the advantages of hearing the (preaching of the) 'True Doctrine' is to be presented.

This has been said by the Exalted One

1 "He who sees the Norm, preached by me, Vakkali, it is he who sees me. For not seeing the Norm, one cannot see me, although he sees me."

The knowledge of the Norm has been placed by the Exalted One himself exactly in the same position as his own. This Norm, however, has been honoured, esteemed, revered and respected by all the Buddhas—past, present and future. He who honours, esteems, reveres and respects the 'Good Norm,' it is he who honours, esteems, reveres, and respects the Exalted One. This has also been said by the Exalted One

2 & 3 "For the destruction of grief of the many, those who were the Sambuddhas in the past, those who are the Sambuddhas at present, and those who will be the Buddhas in the future, they all, paying esteem to the Norm, lived, live and will live respectively. This is the law of the Buddhas.

4 Therefore a lover of oneself wishing for greatness, should esteem the Norm, remembering the teaching of the Buddhas.

5 The Sambuddhas have a twofold body, one the glorious visible body and the other called the body of Norm, the Norm preached by them.

6 Abiding therein by their supernormal powers and knowing fully the syllables, words, name and sense of (the Norm) they obtained the Bodhi-seed.

7 There having been many merits in the Good Norm, a wise person who seeks their welfare should have a peaceful mind and due respect for the Norm.

8 Leaving aside your own work, you have come here to hear (the preaching) of the Norm. Therefore the Norm, preached by the Sambuddha, should be respectfully heard."

Once upon a time, the Exalted One dwelt near Sāvatthi. At that time, in an assembly hall, the venerable Nandaka instructed, roused, incited and delighted the bhikkhus on a doctrinal topic in polite speech, distinct, clearly enunciated, and instructive. And those bhikkhus were hearing attentively the preaching of the Norm in good thought, fixing their mind, pondering and reflecting on it. Now, when the Teacher had finished his preaching of the sermon to a great crowd, taken his meal and comforted his body for a while, he bathed well with water prepared by his attendants, and being properly dressed and covered, went to the door of the assembly hall for the purpose of hearing the preaching of the Norm by the venerable Nanda, and there he, taking hold of the loose pulling rope (of the door) and hearing the preaching of the Norm, remained standing till third watch of the night, and as soon as the preaching was finished he shouted applause, saying "Nanda, the disquisition on the Norm, has been well delivered." And as soon as the Teacher shouted applause, the earthly Nāgas, Supannas, and Yakkhas as well as the earthly gods shouted applause even in one voice reaching up to the Brahma-world. On hearing this, the thera understood: 'This is the sound of the Teacher's applause And instantly he descended in haste from the preacher's seat, and came out. And placing his head on the feet of Him having the Ten Powers, and paying homage to the Exalted One, he said "Reverend Sir, Exalted One, when did you come here?" "I came here, Nanda, when you had just begun (the preaching of) the Suttanta " The thera got frightened, and said "Reverend Sir, Buddha, what you did was indeed hard, you are delicate. That 'I should know the very Tathāgata' even such a thought, therefore, did not occur to me." "Nanda, even when I was fulfilling the Perfectionary virtues for a long period of more than one hundred thousand kappas and four Asaṅkheyyas for the purpose of mastering this good Norm, and when I was fulfilling these virtues in the life of Vidhura, Mahāgovinda, Kuddāloka, Aruka, Jotipāla, Bodhi the mendicant, Mahosadha the wise, and the like, preaching this Norm to others, and was reaching the Perfection of Wisdom, there was no limit of my fulfilling those virtues. At that time, whenever I preached the Norm to others or heard others preach it, I had no satisfaction." To explain this, he said

9 "In immeasurable time, when I was going through different existences, I had no satisfaction, whenever I preached or heard the Norm.

10 Why is it, then, that although at the present time I become a Sambuddha, who is omniscient and an abode of compassion, I have no satisfaction whenever I preach the Norm to the world.

11 Because of my resolve 'Being the Enlightened One, I will enlighten (others).' I am born as a Sambuddha Verily, let me enlighten the beings.

12 Because of my resolve 'Having crossed, I will help (others) to cross over I have overcome suffering Verily, let me help the beings to overcome

13 Because of my resolve 'Being free I will help (others) to be free.' I am free from suffering Verily, let me help the beings to be free.'

14 This Norm has been expounded by the great Sambuddhas. With one's heart inclined

towards the Norm, the best Norm should be heard."

So, precious is this Norm. "In this world of living beings, Nanda, should you be able to preach (the doctrine) for a Kappa, I would also live and hear it for not less than a Kappa," said the Exalted One. The venerable Nandaka, hearing it, said: "wonderful it is Reverend Sir, it is marvellous, Reverend Sir, that the Tathāgata who has himself known all things to be known, who has found out the Path which was not found out, who has known the Path which was not known, who has explained the Path which was not explained, who knows the Path, who is skilled in the Path, thus did not find even satisfaction or exhaustion whenever he himself preached this good Norm or heard others preach it." Knowing thus, this good Norm should be respectfully heard. This preaching (of the Norm) to Nandaka is the first.

The good Norm should respectfully be heard in this world by all those respectable persons who come from different seats (positions) and sit down together and assemble in the preaching hall Here certain preacher of the Norm thinks "The people will know, This is a preacher of the Norm," and thus moving in his desire for gain and honour, he preaches the Norm This does not bear much reward. Some in expectation of their own experiences, preach the Norm to others. This bears much reward, this constitutes an item contributing to the meritorious action of preaching (of the Norm). Some one as he listens there, thinks 'The people will thus know me to be faithful,' and thus moving in his desire for gain and honour, he hears the preaching (of the Norm) This does not bear much reward. Some one again thinks: 'This hearing (of the preaching) of the Norm will be to my great advantage,' and he, wishing for his own welfare, hears (the preachig of) the Norm with a very tender heart inclined towards hearing (of the preaching) of the Norm. This constitutes an item contributing to the meritorious action of hearing (the preaching of the Norm). In this connection, in order to show the advantage of hearing respectfully and of giving one's approval at the time of hearing (the preaching) of the Norm, this is the story

In Sāvatthi, it is said, the husband of a daughter of a certain wealthy man hearing the preaching of the Norm of the Teacher, thought: "It is not possible for me, as a householder, to fulfil this Norm I will renounce the world." He went to a monastery and was ordained before a certain (bhikkhu) who lived on alms-food. When Pasenadi of Kosala had known 'This (lady) is without her husband,' he caused her to be brought into his harem. Then one day a person, taking a bunch of blue lotuses, entered the harem on some business, and presented them to the king. Now the king taking the bunch of blue lotuses, distributed one to each of those women. The flowers having been distributed, that lady, stretching forth her both hands, showed herself cheerful, but when she had scented, she cried out. The king noticing both of her actions sent for her and asked (the reasons) In course of relating the reasons for her becoming cheerful and having a cry, she said :

15 " Here permeates a scent from the mouth of my husband, who is a thera. When I remember him as the lotus, I cry out, O lord of charioteers.

16 His breathing (in and out), full of pleasant smell, blows out. Early he did meritorious deeds, O king. As I had remembered it, I cried out."

Although this was said even for the third time, the king could not believe. Next day, when he caused all garlands, toilet perfumes, and other scented objects to be removed from the entire palace, and had seats prepared for the Order of bhikkhus headed by the Buddha, he invited the Order of bhikkhus headed by the Buddha. When they were seated on those seats, he gave them a great gift

And when they had finished taking their meals, he asked that lady : " Which thera ? " " This thera, lord." Then the king, paying homage to the Teacher, said : " Reverend Sir, Let the Order of bhikkhus go along with you, let such and such thera make the act of approval." Then the

Teacher, leaving that bhikkhu, went to the monastery. Thereafter as soon as the thera began the act of approval, the entire palace was filled as if with the perfumes of scent, camphor, sandal, and the residue of sesamum oil. The king thought: "This lady speaks truly," and became glad. Next day, he asked the Teacher about its reason. Then the Exalted One explained: "O great king, formerly when this man was hearing the preaching of the Norm, his body was touched by the fivefold joy and his hairs stood erect. When his body was filled with that joy, a sound: ''Tis well!, 'Tis well!' came out of his mouth, and while shouting applause, he heard (the preaching of) the Norm. For that reason, O great king, he acquired this merit."

As it has been said

17 "At the time of preaching the good Norm he who says ''Tis well, 'Tis well,' good smell spreads from his mouth, as does from the lotus in the water.

18 Uttered pleasantly were the utterances of the Sambuddhas. He who praises highly this pleasant Norm, becomes a wise man full of sweet voice having his mouth well perfumed and uttering a sweet cry.

Because one sees this merit of hearing respectfully (the preaching of the Norm), he should hear (the preaching of) the good Norm with due respect. (This account of) shouting applause is the second

19 Let those of you who have come here and taken seats together for the purpose of hearing (the preaching of) the good Norm, hear that Norm with a peaceful heart."

Once upon a time the Teacher, the Exalted One, was residing at Sāvatthi in the Jetavana with his excellent Order. At that time the Buddha, honoured by Brāhmaṇas and gods, delivered this discourse

"Gifts, O brethren, are of two kinds. Which are the two? Material gifts and spiritual gifts. These, bhikkhus, are the two kinds of gifts Of these two, brethren, this is the best, namely, spiritual gifts." [1]

This Norm means mindfulness and right exertion. This Norm is called the basis of Iddhi, the controlling faculties, the constituents of higher knowledge, the eightfold Path, Insight into the Aryan Truth, a lamp for the highest reward in Nibbāna But in this world, whosoever wishing for merit, speaks consistently of any one of the nine classes of the texts, the Sutta, the Geyya, and the rest, he, being indifferent to his gain and even respecting the good Norm, teaches either the Sutta or the Vedalla This gift of the doctrine is called the best gift. Should any one offer fine and costly robes, in a sufficient number, resembling the spathes of plaintain trees to the Buddhas,

[1] *Anguttara-Nikāya*, Vol II, p 13

the Paccekabuddhas and to those who are free from the āsavas, who are always seated cross-legged in the interior of the Cakkavāla sphere extending up to the Brahma-world, even an approval in a gāthā of four half-lines for the purpose of approving of the gift in that congregation, is the superior (to such gift) Why? (Because) this gift is not worth an infinitesimal portion of that gāthā. In preaching the Norm thus, he spoke of its merit Or, again, as to the great merit · a person who makes (others) hear (the preaching of) the Norm, is said to acquire a great merit. Again, even a gift of the doctrine given there, in that congregation, in a gāthā of four half-lines, by way of approval, is superior to a gift of excellent food prepared from the best kind of grains with meat and with various kinds of soup and curry, and offered after filling the bowels with it to such a company; or even to a gift of medicine, complete with ghee, fresh butter, oil, honey, sugar, molasses, and the like; or even to a gift of seats and beds offered after constructing many hundred thousand vihāras like the Mahāvihāra and mansions like the Lohapāsāda, or to a gift made at a cost of fifty-four kotis (coins), even as did the householder Anāthapiṇḍika buy a land for the price of (lit. by spreading out) eighty koti (coins) for the purpose of constructing the Jetavana vihāra, build a mansion at a cost of eighty kotis (coins), and honour the vihāra spending eighty kotis (coins), or, likewise, to a gift of twenty-seven kotis (coins), even as did the great female lay-devotee Visākhā, in the construction of a mansion in Pubbārāma, buy a land for the price of nine kotis, build the mansion at a cost of nine koṭis, and honour the vihāra spending nine kotis Why? Those rich Khattiyas and Brāhmanas who perform such meritorious actions, do these after hearing (the preaching of) the Norm and not without hearing it. Had not these beings heard (the preaching of) the Norm, they would not have given even a spoonful of ricegruel or even a ladleful of rice. It is for this reason that only the gift of the doctrine is the best of all gifts.

Moreover, excepting the Buddhas, and the Paccekabuddhas, others like Sāriputta and the rest, who possessed the knowledge by which they could count even drops of water if the rains were to set in for an entire Kappa, were unable to attain the Path of a Stream-Winner, the Fruit thereof and the rest by their own capacity to the Norm. The thera Assaji and others realised the Fruit of a Stream-Winner, after hearing the Norm preached; they realised the knowledge of the Perfectionary virtues of a disciple by the Teacher's preaching of the Norm Even the thera Sāriputta, when he had heard the Exalted One preach the Norm, acquired the sixteen kinds of knowledge along with the Path to Arahantship. He had intelligence in hearing; he had abundant, developed, great, wide, deep, complete, extensive, full, rapid, easy-going, quick, alert, sharp, penetrating wisdom, he was endowed with the knowledge of Perfectionary virtues of a disciple. It is for this reason that only the gift of the doctrine is deemed to be the best, chief, excellent and first of all gifts

Even imagining of this gift, when Sakka, king of gods, being at the head of gods of ten thousand Cakkavālas, had approached the Teacher and paid homage to the Exalted One, he asked "Reverend Sir, among the gifts, which is the best; among tastes, which is the best, on what grounds the destruction of desire is the foremost?" Then the Teacher, in giving answer to his four questions, uttered this verse:

20 "A gift of the doctrine excels all gifts, the taste of Dhamma excels all tastes, the delight in Dhamma excels all delights, the destruction of desire surpasses all sufferings"

When the teacher had thus spoken the answer of the four questions in this verse, eighty-four thousand gods realised the Norm. When Sakka had heard the Teacher's discourse on the Norm, he paid homage to the Teacher and said

"Reverend Sir, why do you not grant us a gift of merit even in the matter of the doctrine which is thus known as the foremost? It would be well, Reverend Sir, that henceforth you should speak to the Order of bhikkhus and grant us a gift of merit." Having said thus and paid homage to the Tathāgata, and gone round thrice with folded hands keeping him to his left, he departed to the deva-world with his company Then the Teacher, when that night had passed away, assembled the Order of bhikkhus and said thus · "O Bhikkhus, henceforth, after you have spoken on the occasion of a great hearing (of the preaching) of the Norm, or of an ordinary hearing (of the preaching) of the Norm, or of making discourse by sitting, or of making even an approval, you should give a gift of merit to all beings." When he had thus spoken, the Order of bhikkhus consented, saying "It is well, Reverend Sir." From that day even up to the present time they make a gift of merit to all beings Thus knowing the good qualities of the Buddha and with a heartfelt faith in the Buddha, the Exalted One, the good Norm should be preached and heard. (This account of) spiritual gift is the third.

21 "Leaving aside your own work, you have come here to hear (the preaching of) the Norm Therefore the Norm, preached by the Sambuddha, should be respectfully heard.

22 The wise who listen to what was sung and uttered by women about old age, disease and death, obtain the highest reward."

How? Formerly, it is said, during a Buddha-interval, a certain person entered a forest with his seven sons. After having finished the work which was to be done, during day-time, as he was returning from the forest in the evening, he heard a certain woman who, in front of her own door, having filled a mortar with paddy, had been grinding it with a pestle and winnowing it with a little sieve, singing :

23 "This paddy, broken with a pestle and free from chaffs, lies here as mere rice. Look at this bodily form which, when broken with old age, is only a skeleton

24 This (bodily form) crushed by old age, is supported by the dried up skin and flesh This is split asunder by death, this is a food eaten by the king of Death This is an abode of worms, and is filled with various corpses This is a dish of impurity, this is unsubstantial like a trunk of the plantain tree

25 This paddy is broken with a pestle. This body is broken by death. Look, look at the (bodily) form which is broken up, broken up by birth, old age and death "

On hearing this song, when he, on reflection, had led up to the three things, namely, impermanence, ill, and non-soul, he with his sons attained the Paccekabuddhahood then and there.

Now, when they were invited by the people at evening time · "Take this food," they replied · "We do not take food after noon, we are Paccekabuddhas." "Lord, the Paccekabuddhas are not like you." "Then what are they like?"

"They having cut off their hair and beard, and having covered themselves with yellow robes. become unattached either to a family or to a company, and they, like the clouds severed by the wind, or like the moon free from the eclipse, live in the caves at the foot of the Nanda forest in the Himalayas. Such are the Paccekabuddhas, O sires."

At that moment they all raised their hands upwards, and touched their heads. Instantly, the characteristics of a lay man disappeared, (and) the characteristics of a recluse became manifest (in them). All of them were holding the eight requisites and waistbands. When they, standing in the air, had admonished a great crowd, they went to the cave at the foot of the Nanda forest in the Northern Himalayas through the air.

Thus the wise men, having heard the teaching included in the song, that is, impermanence, ill and non-soul, became thereby bringers of riddance and bliss. Knowing this, the Ancients therefore said to this effect :

26 "Without considering birth, lineage, family and beauty (of a person) the wise ones should make the Norm firm and hear (the preaching of) the best Norm A wise man without caring for the colour of a cow, should examine the milk, produced in a cow, for the milk is the best of all tastes. Likewise, the good Norm, whoever preaches it, should be heard with due honour, the

Norm being preached by the Sambuddha After hearing the Norm from the Sambuddha, all that is preached to others or explained to them, is what was preached by the Buddha "

Knowing this fact, one should hear with due honour the good Norm (This account of) Dhaññakotthita is the fourth.

27 " Leaving aside your own work, you have come here to hear (the preaching of) the Norm. Therefore the Norm preached by the Sambuddha should be respectfully heard."

28 " Let the wise ones hear what was sung and uttered by women about old age, disease and death, and let them obtain the highest reward."

How ? To explain the matter, this is the story :

In the island of Sīhala, it is said, there was a village inhabited by a great multitude. Not far from that village, there was a large pond, full of (blue) lotuses. At that time a female slave moved about, keeping watch over it Having found the lotuses full-blown in that very pond, she would come down, and while breaking the lotuses, she would sing a song in this manner

29 " Look at this very beautiful lotus, covered and obstructed by its hairy structures. So long as its fading nature does not overcome it in this way, it looks beautiful and diffuses a sweet smell."

So she said. On hearing the voice of her song, a carrier of "currey leaf," who was gathering flowers from the branches of a Talambaka tree, while singing after that song, said

30 "Look here at this very beautiful person (*kāya*) bearing only the youth. So long as old age does not overcome it, it looks beautiful and makes a gesture of merriment"

On hearing this, the lotus plant thought "She speaks right, I should now relate the true nature of these lotuses, and I will again speak about this person." Having understood this, she spoke thus :

31 "This person, adorned with the tender leaves, shines glorious and delightful. So long as its fading nature does not overcome it, it looks beautiful and diffuses a sweet smell."

The green leaf replied

32 "She is intoxicated, she is intoxicated with the pride of beauty, and does not seek for her welfare in this world So long as old age does not overcome it, it looks beautiful and makes a gesture of merriment."

The lotus plant rejoined ·

33 "The sun is up, the pollens are bloomed. The bees sing delightfully. So long as its fading nature does not overcome it, it looks beautiful, and emits a sweet smell."

The green leaf, while giving a reply to that lotus plant, said :

34 "The open and blossomed lotus is spurred by the sunshine, even so the beings, born as men, are moved by the pressure of old age'

At that time only sixty bhikkhus practising endurance lived in a suitable place near that village. All of them, lost in concentration, always quiet, and acting rightly day and night, would live mindful of their objects of meditation in walking, in sitting, and in all postures of the body each of them thinking "Even this very day I will attain and realise Arahantship." On that day in early morning when they had dressed themselves, and taken their bowls and upper garments, they while going to the village for alms along the path, heard the voice of their songs. And the thera addressing all the bhikkhus, said "Friends, what has been spoken by these is true. Like a blossomed lotus the person of all beings is indeed delightful for a moment." And even standing there, he, while enlightening them, said

35 "There must have been such a palpable drawback in one's very origin. Similarly, this body looks beautiful at first, but when it comes to old age, it is withered like a lotus."

When he had said this, he spoke thus. "Friends, all constituents of existence are subject to decay and are of uncertain nature. It is proper even to get wearied of all constituents, it is proper to set oneself free from passion, it is proper to be emancipated." When they, all coming into an emotion, had set up their developed objects of thought and cultivated insight, they attained Arahantship including analytic insight then and there. The thera, having understood that those bhikkhus had attained Arahantship together with himself, said thus:

36 "This bodily aggregate is a conditioned thing, impermanent, without a soul, an abode of birth, old age, falling away and disease, and has the nature of many sufferings. Leaving it aside, let one come to bliss."

So saying, he went away with them. Thus the good men having heard what is known as the good Norm of the Tathāgata, whoever preaches it, and even having mastered the song of the female slave and having heard the Norm, become bringers of their own riddance and bliss. It is for this reason that the good Norm should be heard. (This account of the song of the green-leaf is the fifth.)

37 "Leaving aside your own work, you have come here to hear (the preaching of) the Norm. Therefore the Norm preached by the Sambuddha should be respectfully heard."

Why speak of those who are born as men, who know good and no good, moral and immoral, just and unjust? Even those who were born as animals, to wit, frogs, owls, bats, deer, fish, *Ajagaras* (Boa constrictors), rats, snakes, and the like, who had no knowledge of anything, they, too, even on hearing the sound of proclamation of the Norm, only repeated by others, were pleased with that sound of proclamation. And when they had passed away making the voice an object of their thought, they brought their own highest happiness in the next existence. Here the story of a frog is to be related first As for the frog, this is the connected story

Once upon a time, it is said, the Exalted One was staying on the bank of a pond of Gaggarā in the city of Campakā. Now one evening, the Exalted One preached the Norm to the inhabitants of Campakā. Then a frog who had gone there, made the Exalted One's voice as an object of its thought. A cow-herd who stood there leaning on a stick, pressed its head Instantly, the frog died and, as one awakened from sleep, it, attended by a company of the celestial nymphs, was reborn in the Tāvatimsa sphere, in a golden celestial abode measuring twelve yojanas in extent Subsequently it looked at its own life and on reflection · "I am born here, what did I do ?" It found nothing but its making the Exalted One's voice an object of its thought Instantly, it came down with its celestial abode and paid homage at the feet of the Exalted One The Exalted One, while enquiring inspite of his knowledge, uttered this verse on that occasion

38 "Who is that, shining in the supernormal Power and in glory, and radiating all directions

with an unsurpassed beauty, that pays homage at my feet?"

The god addressed the Exalted One in a verse:

39 "Formerly, I was a frog in water, and lived in water. As I was hearing the Norm preached by you, a cow-herd killed me."

The Exalted One preached him the Norm. At the end of the preaching, eighty-four thousand beings had the realisation of the Norm. When the god, also placed on the Fruit of Stream-winner, had gone round in reverence, keeping the Exalted One to his left side, he went away to a heaven. Knowing the significance, however, a wise man, who seeks for his own welfare, should respectfully hear the good Norm. (This) account of a frog is the sixth.

40 "Leaving aside your own work, you have come here to hear (the preaching of) the Norm. Therefore the good Norm preached by the Sambuddha should be respectfully heard."

As for the bats, this is the connected story.

Once upon a time, it is said, when in expounding the Abhidhamma in heaven, going beyond the world of men and producing a created Buddha resembling the Sammā-Sambuddha for preaching the Norm among the assemblies of gods, he came down from heaven, and when coming down, he made use of water in the lake Anotatta and reared his body, at that time he taught the venerable

Sāriputta, who had attended the Exalted One, those units of Dhamma which were expounded in heaven. Sāriputta, too, having learnt the entire Abhidhamma-piṭaka and codified it in front of the Buddha, repeated it at the entrance of a certain cave. When the five hundred bats, who resided there, had grasped only the sound of that voice and fixed that sound as an object of their thought, they, not knowing even the sense of the Dhamma, pondered: "This sound does not press us, nor make us understand. Therefore, those sounds which produce a desire for worldly passions, kill the beings, and are followed by separation, are all harsh, very evil, and not pleasing. This Buddha is charming, worth hearing, and affectionate." Having pondered thus, they made the Dhamma an object of their thought, and without seeking for food, passed away even there. By the power of hearing (the preaching of) the Norm those bats were reborn in heaven, each having a company of five hundred thousand (gods) and a golden celestial abode, twelve yojanas in extent, resounding with various sorts of dancing, singing and music by the celestial nymphs. At the moment of their taking rebirth when the king of gods together with the companies of gods had honoured them with the celestial incenses, perfumes, garlands and the rest, in order to show them respect, he said thus.

41 "(To have) comrades like you in heaven is indeed a joy. Besides, as you were born among

men, you have been on a footing for a long time.

42 And the disciples you must be of the Buddha, the pure. On hearing the Norm, preached by Sāriputta, you will enter into Nibbāna."

So saying, he again bowed down. All the bat-gods, having experienced the joy in heaven for a long time, passed away, and were reborn in the families of Brāhmaṇas and householders. When they had grown up as comrades of each other, they heard Sāriputta preaching the Norm, and entered the Order. When they had learnt the Abhidhamma-Piṭaka and the commentary thereon with their well-intoned speech, and had developed insight shortly after, they became free from the sufferings of existence and destroyed their āsavas Those disciples of the Buddha, excepting Sāriputta, who had first learnt the Abhidhamma-Piṭaka and the commentary thereon with their well-intoned speech, they all became known in this world as comrades of each other like the bat-gods. Because of their abundant faith in the Norm, they, having thus heard only the intoning of voice, experienced joy in heaven till their attainment of Nibbāna.

To this effect it has been said .

43 & 44 "Why speak of him who, having learnt the whole meaning (of the Piṭaka), repeats it ? He who honours it in faith, speaking about the enumeration of its name, comes nearer to one who has mastered a well-intoned speech in respect

of the text, in a future existence, as a result of the act done."

Thus it has been said by the Exalted One:

45 "Leave aside the question of one who knows the syllables and the words. I gained the Bodhi-seed through my knowledge of name and sense.

46 At the sound of the voice of the bhikkhus who were expounding the Abhidhamma, the bats, too, were delighted, and while rejoicing, they went to heaven.

47 He who, having preached and honoured the Abhidhamma, pays homage, reaches a blissful and happy world, and afterwards comes to Nibbāna.

48 And those, who have taken refuge in the order of the Sakyan Lion, obtain such a footing, after hearing the Norm of the great Sage

49 Those who make Dhamma an object of their thought, and rejoice with a faithful heart, no doubt, experience the advantages of hearing (the preaching of) the Norm."

Knowing this matter, however, a wise man, who seeks his own welfare, should respectfully hear the good Norm. (This) account of bats is the seventh.

As for the young deer, this is the connected story:

In the island of Sīhala, it is said, there was a beautiful vihāra named Uddalolaka. At that time many a deer, pigs, and the like lived in that vihāra-park. Now, in a certain village, when a hunter's son had seen many deer and pigs there, had made a room at one side, and had tied up leaves in the boundary of the forest, he stood in the room, taking up his bow and quiver and looking forward to the approach of the deer. Now, when a deer had taken his food here and there, he, while going to a landing place to drink water, heard the sound proclaimed for hearing (the preaching of) the Norm on the spot of that hermitage, and he stood there with his neck stretched out, ears raised, eyes wide open, and feet lifted up, making the voice of the preacher of the Norm an object of his thought. At that very moment the hunter hit him with a single stroke and caused him death. Now, the deer, after his death, took his rebirth in the womb of the younger sister of the great thera Abhaya, a resident of that vihāra. When, after the lapse of ten months, he had come out of his mother's womb, he, while growing up gradually, was seven years of age. Thereafter his parents took him to thera Abhaya. The latter was not long in giving him ordination. The young boy, however, attained Arahantship even on a razor-touch, through the power of his hearing (the preaching of) the Norm, when formerly he was born as a deer. But his maternal uncle, the thera, then attained only the five abhiññā, and had not won the Path of an Arahant.

Now, one day, the Sāmanera went to this religious teacher. Then his teacher stretching forth his hands, crushed the disc of the moon as it were. The Sāmaṇera, seeing it, said. "Reverend Sir, this ought to be saved." The thera, however, not knowing the fact of his (the Sāmanera's) being placed on Arahantship, the highest Fruit, did not carefully consider his words. Then the Sāmaṇera, fetching one thousand moons by his supernormal power, showed them to the thera and said:

"Reverend sir, it is not difficult to fetch one hundred moons, one thousand moons, or one hundred thousand moons. But he who eliminates a single desire, is indeed the best. This is indeed difficult." When he had said this, he spoke thus:

50 "A person who goes to a bank, and even while standing on it, sees a great mass of water, says unwisely: 'I have seen this ocean.'

51 & 52 Even so, in this world, a bhikkhu who only gives up some of his own lusts, obtains the impermanent power of abhiññās, and does not destroy (all) lusts, considers himself 'I have obtained my wishes.' Because of his slavery to desires, he indeed is not free.

53 A bhikkhu, who gives up the unlucky, unhappy, dreadful, constantly flowing, and harmful desires, is free from the bondage of Māra."

The thera, hearing this, won Arahantship even on the same day. Next day, the younger sister of the thera invited the thera together with the Sāmanera The thera spoke to his sister thus: "Upāsikā, you ought to gladden your heart this day at the sight of many bhikkhus. But let the share (of food) be (ready) for both of us." When (the thera) had sent her back, he, having dressed himself in the forenoon and taking his bowl and upper garment, came with some thirty-thousand bhikkhus. She, seeing this, prepared two seats for the uncle and the nephew. These became as many as thirty-thousand through their power. Even through their power her house was enlarged. The bhikkhus were seated in their respective seats. The soup, curry, and the like, all that she had prepared for two persons, was enough for as many as thirty thousand bhikkhus, and as far as they needed. When they had finished their meal, the female lay devotee took the bowl of the Sāmanera in order to get the meal approved (by him). In their midst, he, too, while increasing the blessing and uttering sweet voice, preached the Norm When the sermon was finished, five hundred families, consisting of father, mother, and the rest, found a support in the Fruit of a Stream-Winner. This preaching was profitable to many people.

54 "When (the Norm) is thus preached, the wood-born deer which grasp the Norm, even making the sound an object of their thought, attain the wealth of the human life and the final

liberation. A wise man established in faith in the Buddha, having heard the Norm well, delights in this world, nay, in heaven in a celestial abode, describable by a sage."

(This) account of a young deer is the eighth.

55 "Leaving aside your own work, you have come here to hear the Norm. Therefore the Norm, preached by the Sambuddha, should be respectfully heard."

As for a fish, this is the connected story :

Once upon a time, many merchants, desirous of going to the island of Lankā, took a sea-going ship. When they had equipped the ship with the various kinds of goods and had filled it with other provisions, such as sesame, rice and the like, they started under the constellation of Bhaddā. At that time a bhikkhu, desirous of going to the other shore with them, asked the merchants for a room for himself, and when they had given him a room, he entered it and was seated. Then the ship, evenly borne by the wind, went on peacefully. Even being seated there, the bhikkhu, while mastering thoroughly his study, recited a portion of (the chapter, called) 'Rise of consciousness' thus. "Things are moral, immoral and unmoral They are associated with a feeling which is either pleasant or painful or neither pleasant nor painful"

When a great fish, which was moving there by one side of the ship, had heard only the sound of the voice of the bhikkhu's recitation, it became pleased with that sound, and did not make up its mind to go elsewhere. Having but one intention there it followed the ship closely at its back, keeping, however, both of its ears motionless. While following the ship as far as the landing place, it had its thought attracted by the hearing of the sound. Then struck by the people standing on the bank of the landing place, it died then and there.

In the island of Sīhala. there was a country known as Rohinī Reborn in a wealthy family there, he grew up with great supremacy and good company. Since at the birth-time of the young boy, his relatives were pleased and delighted, they named him Sumana-Tissa. But in that house, the bhikkhus, attended by his parents, would regularly take their food. By constant look, the young boy was pleased with their conduct and living, and even when he came of age, he, leaving aside such wealth, wished to be initiated. Although he was entreated by his parents in many ways, he did not pay heed to their words, and even while they were crying and lamenting, he made them give permission for his initiation, as did the sons of Raṭṭhapāla. From the time of his initiation he, while in a Sāmaṇera-stage, mastered thoroughly the entire Suttanta-Pitaka and Abhidhamma-Pitaka, and during his ordination period, he, having mastered the entire Vinaya-Pitaka, became versed in the three Pitakas Because of his initiation through faith, he was known as the faithful thera Sumana-Tissa. Like the moon resting in the expanse of the heavens, he was renowned and had a great company He arrived at the island of Nāga for the purpose of worshiping the Great Cetiya And there in the beautiful garden of Mūlgiri, assembled the Order of bhikkhus who were fond of delighting in seclusion and devoted to contemplation On seeing it, when the thera, gladdened at heart, had been pleased and had cooled his hands and feet, he was seated cross-legged near a tree, making the Buddha an object of his thought. And as soon as he directed his thought, he attained Arahantship, the highest fruit, even though by a voice as his one object of thought, he became worthy of the highest gift of the world By what, however, was this Arahantship given? It was given by the hearing of the Norm with due respect.

To this effect the Ancients said

56 "And those fishes living in water, which had heard the Norm recited, and had been sympathetic by that voice, when reborn, reached emancipation"

Therefore, the good Norm should be respectfully heard. (This) account of the faithful thera Sumana is the ninth.

57 "Leaving aside your own work, you have come here to hear the Norm Therfore the Norm,

preached by the Sambuddha, should be respectfully heard ''

As for the Ajagara-serpent, this is the connected story·

In the time of Kassapa, the Sammāsambuddha, it is said, some one was reborn as an *Ajagara*-serpent. Having approached the bhikkhus, versed in the Abhidhamma, he lay down. As they were reciting a discourse on the sphere of senses, he, having made the voice an object of his thought, died, and was reborn in heaven. Even in heaven, he experienced the bliss till the attainment of the Parinibbāna by our Teacher. When the Exalted One had attained the Parinibbāna, he was, however, reborn in a Brāhmana family. When he came of age, he took the vow of an ājīvaka mendicant, and became the family-priest of the chief consort of king Bindusāra

At that time four kinds of longing of a pregnant woman were manifest in that lady. Which were the four? (These were·) Longing to eat the light of the stars, after treading upon the sun and the moon; longing to eat the clouds; longing to eat earth-worms; longing to eat trees which drink with feet and breathe with leaves.

Therefore Ājīvaka explained to the king the means by which her longings would be allayed. In that connection, the king was cleverly informed. Being asked, 'Why are (these) longings manifest in the queen?', He explained, 'O great king, this queen will get a beautiful prince, perfect in all respects.' When he, desirous of explaining in detail the meaning of her longings, had approached the queen, he was seated on a costly seat assigned by her. Being enquired by the queen, 'What is the matter?', he replied, "I have something to say I did not say it to the enemies in the midst of the royal assembly Now I have come to say this to you "

When she had said, 'Sir, please speak, we shall hear it," he spoke, "O queen, I will speak only about your getting a son, not anything else. Now hear it." "O queen. your son," continued he, "will be a king. Your longing for treading upon the sun and the moon forecasts that in the whole of Jambudīpa, there will be one hundred kings serving at his feet, your longing to eat the light of stars is a foregoing sign of his act of killing his brother who will be just an unpleasant heir to him; your longing to eat the clouds is a foregoing sign of his exertion just for (the growth of) the excellent Sāsana of the Sambuddha, after destroying ninety-six sects who will come into disputation with him, your longing to eat trees which drink with feet and breathe with leaves, is a foregoing sign of his issuing orders extending one yojana above in the air" And thus when he had related all portents and results of her longing, he said. "You have got such longing because of your getting the very son, bear this in mind." Highly delighted at this, she said: "If those (good) results are accomplished, I will fetch you in a golden palanquin from your dwelling place." She paid him reverence, and while establishing a connection with him, asked his name, caused it to be written in a golden plate, and took leave of him. Subsequently, the ceremony for the protection of her embryo being duly performed, she gave birth in due time and got a son.

Now one day, the king caused that boy to sit down on his lap, and while making him play, he took his seat. Some other people having brought a precious shell, the spiral of which turned to the right, placed it on the king's hand. The young boy let loose the precious stone. So the king took him with the precious shell and besprinkled over the boy's head. And the queen, seeing this, was angry and took the boy from his hands, and informed this matter to her own family-priest. The latter explained: "O queen, surely this son of yours will be the highest king in the whole of Jambudīpa." And when he, honoured by her, had gone one hundred yojanas therefrom, he lived in a certain place. Now in course of time, when Dhammāsoka had suppressed his enemies and had ascended the throne after his father's death, he, one day, asked his mother: "Mother, was this fortune of ours predicted formerly or not?" She replied: "Dear son, we have a family-priest who predicted such thing."

On hearing "In what, mother, wherein does he live?", she said, "Only one hundred yojanas hence." Thinking 'I shall honour the teacher,' he sent his men with a golden palanquin for him. While being carried by them, he (the priest) noticed, on his way, the dwelling place of the thera Assagutta in Vattaniya-senāsana. Thinking 'This must be the dwelling place of the recluses,' he descended from the palanquin and went on foot to that place, when he had seen the lions, tigers, hyænas, large species of deer, pigs, deer (in general), and the like, which had been formerly bent on annoying one other, united in a harmonious group with kindly thought, through the power of love of the thera, and when he had also seen the thera serving them with water, he asked the thera: "What are these?" While examining his fortune, the thera found that it had been due to the fact of hi formerly hearing a discourse on the *āyatanas*, and thinking "Let the very thing be his assurance (of the goal)," he replied "These are called *āyatanas* (exertions), friend." He asked. "What are the doings of these?", and was replied in that connection: "The very exertions are their doings." And even as he heard this, he was taken by shame and fear of sin and he was seated in the posture of squatting. The thera gave him a bathing mantle. Then he, having asked for initiation, became initiated in the presence of the thera. When he had accepted a particular formula regarding the object of his thought (from his teacher), had developed an insight, and had ended all ill of transmigration, he reached Arahantship, the highest fruit. But by whom was this Arahantship given? Was it not given by the hearing of the Norm with due respect?

To this effect said the Ancients :

58 "On hearing the Norm recited, the *ajagara*-serpent who was delighted with that voice, passed away (from that existence to the other), and then attained emancipation."

Therefore the good Norm should be respectfully heard. (This) account of an *ajagara*-serpent is the tenth.

59 "Leaving aside your own work, you have come here to hear the Norm. Hence, the Norm, preached by the Sambuddha, should be respectfully heard"

As for the rat-snake, this is the connected story :

When the great king Kākavaṇṇa-Tissa was reigning in Mahāgāma in the Rohana country in the island of Lankā, the thera Mahādhammadinna, a resident of the Talangaratissa mountain, was staying in the Devarakkhita cave. At that time there was a great ant-hill near this cave. There in the ant-hill, a rat-snake lived, taking his food wherever he pleased As time went on thus, one day, while he was taking his food, (they) destroyed his both eyes Being afflicted with pain and unable to take his food outside the ant-hill, he lay there. Thereafter the thera, seeing the rat-snake afflicted and lying in that way, and being compassionate towards him, stood on the path of his hearing and preached the Norm with the help of the *Mahāsatipatthāna-suttanta* While hearing that Norm, he set up his object of thought in the voice and inclined his heart towards it At the very moment an iguana killed and ate him. By that result (of Kamma) he passed away therefrom, and was reborn in the family of a certain minister of King Dutthagāmini in Anurādhapura. As he grew up, they named him Tissāmacca. He was endowed with the various kinds of wealth, such as gold, money, cows, buffaloes, and servants, male and female, and the like By the mere taking up of a thought-object in a voice, the Norm produces such a great fortune Oh, the power of the good Norm !

As to this, these are the citations

60 " Oh, the power of the Norm of Sugata, the great sage ! It makes him who is born, free from birth and honoured by the world.

61 The Norm always makes a poor man rich, a low-born person to attain the position of a high family and a stupid to attain intelligence.

62 The path to hell is straight and is a thorny fence, while the path to heaven is a well-prepared high road.

63 In avoidance of old age and disease, this good Norm is a sure footing of immortality. Therefore this should be practised reverentially even by a group of people.

64 Therefore one, who hears this lustre of the Norm, attains the human prosperity. Would there be a person wishing for his own good who would not practise that useful Norm?"

Later on, he, having performed many meritorious deeds, passed away, and, as one awakened from sleep, was reborn in a golden celestial abode in the excellent heaven

65 "Let him who is calmed, hear the immortal (Norm) set in motion by the Conqueror, Let him practise, honour and worship it Let him take shelter in it, while standing, walking, lying, and sitting. Let there be always devotion (in him)"

The account of a rat-snake is the eleventh.

Here ends the Chapter, called the 'Account of the Advantages of Hearing (the Preaching of) the Norm' in the *Saddhammasamgaha*, compiled for the serene joy and emotion of the pious.

The Colophon

1 In Sīhala, there was a person who, like the moon, shone in the sphere of the Sāsana, and enlightened the 'water-born' people residing in Lankā with the rays of knowledge

2 His name was Dhammakitti, and he was virtuous and a mine of merits. Like the moon in the sky, he was renowned in the Sīhala island.

3 In the entire Piṭakas, and in grammar, and the like, he reached perfection. He was highly intelligent, and he brightened the island of Lankā.

4 His disciple, famous as Dhammakitti-Mahāsāmī, who had endeavoured to come over to Lankā, reached the delightful Laṅkā.

5 There he, having performed many meritorious deeds and having received the pabbajjā from the thera, returned to his own country, and reached the city of Yodaya.

6 & 7 While staying in a great residence called the Lankārāma, built by the great king named Paramarājā, the eminent master Dhammakitti, pure in conduct, and wise, compiled this (work) called the *Saddhammasaṃgaha* complete in all respects

INDEX